StarLancer

OFFICIAL Strategies & Secrets™

Doug Radcliffe

SYBEX ®

SAN FRANCISCO   PARIS   DÜSSELDORF   SOEST   LONDON

Associate Publisher:	DAN BRODNITZ
Contracts and Licensing Manager:	KRISTINE O'CALLAGHAN
Acquisitions and Developmental Editor:	TORY McLEARN AND DAN BRODNITZ
Managing Editor Game Books:	KARI BROOKS
Editor:	BRETT TODD
Production Editor:	NINA KREIDEN
Associate Production Editor:	KELLY WINQUIST
Proofreader:	LINDY WOLF
Book Design:	MUELLER DESIGN INTERACTIVE
Book Production:	WILLIAM SALIT DESIGN
Production Assistant:	LISA LUSK
Cover Designer:	CALYX DESIGN

To Levi Michael Hopkins and Ryan Dorey, the funniest, most unique and honest guys that I have *never* met. Stay smart and continue to look at life with just enough seriousness.

Acknowledgments

Many thanks to Sybex and its always professional staff. Tory, best wishes on your next venture. Dan, thanks for your continued pats on the back. Kari and Nina, I always appreciated the friendly reminders and helpful suggestions. Thanks to the entire editorial and production crew, including Kyle Mueller, Brett Todd, William Salit, Lisa Lusk, Lindy Wolf, and Kelly Winquist. Thanks to Microsoft, Digital Anvil, and Warthog for creating one of the best space combat simulations ever. I sincerely appreciate the timely help and detailed documents, which made the entire process a pleasure to complete. Special thanks to Robert Lindsley at Microsoft.

A Letter from the Publisher

Dear Reader,

At Sybex, our goal is to bring you the best game strategy guides money can buy. We hire the best authors in the business, and we bring our love of games to the look and feel of the books. We hope you see all of that reflected in the strategy guide you're holding in your hands right now.

The important question is: How well do YOU think we're doing?

Are we providing you with the kind of in-depth, hardcore gaming content you crave? Is the material presented in a way you find both useful and attractive? Are there other approaches and/or types of information you'd like to see but just aren't getting? Or, are our books so perfect that you're considering nominating them for a Pulitzer this year?

Your comments and suggestions are always valuable. We want to encourage even more feedback from our readers and make it even easier for you to get in touch with us. To that end, we've created an e-mailbox for your feedback. We invite you to send your comments, criticism, praise, and suggestions to **gamesfeedback@sybex.com** and let us know what you think.

We can't guarantee we'll respond to every message; but we can promise we'll read them all, take them to heart, and then print them out and use the hard copy to make festive hats for everyone in the building.

Most of all, we'll use your feedback to continuously improve the quality of our books. So please, let us hear from you!

Dan Brodnitz
Associate Publisher

contents

Part 1: alliance academy   1

chapter 1 Flight Training   3

chapter 2 Dogfighting Strategies   15

Part 2: alliance intelligence   27

chapter 3 Ship Strategies and Statistics   29

chapter 4 Weapon Strategies and Statistics 45

contents

chapter 6   Raiders: The Guerrilla War— Missions 8 to 11   93

chapter 7 Frontier Operations—Missions 12 to 16   113

contents

chapter 10   The Sixth Campaign—
 Missions 22 to 24   161

part 4: multiplayer combat   175

chapter 11   Deathmatch Strategies   177

contents

Introduction

War rages across the solar system. Our bases are being systematically destroyed. Our command infrastructure is nonexistent.

We're attempting to regroup at Oberon. The Alliance needs all capable pilots to report to Oberon immediately to form the 45th Volunteer Squadron. The 45th, along with the remnants of what remains of the Alliance fleet, will be our last vanguard.

It will be on Oberon that we make our final stand against the Eastern Coalition fleets. Failure . . . is not an option.

Welcome to the 45th Volunteers. Count yourself lucky to be part of the most patriotic and highly motivated team in the fleet! Don't let being members of the 45th go to your head, though. We've got a tough job to do, so cooperate with the other squadrons. There's plenty of glory out there for everyone!

The 45th has access to state of the art fighters, missiles, gunnery, and a topnotch flight crew to keep you up and running. We'll need them. The Coalition has us outnumbered and our supply lines are strained.

StarLancer is an epic space combat simulation from the designers of *Wing Commander, Strike Commander*, and *Privateer*. Assuming the role of an Alliance pilot, you'll help wage war against the Eastern Coalition for control of key planets and moons in the Sol sector. Across 24 action-packed missions, you'll perform such duties as escorting convoys, attacking starbases, intercepting torpedoes, and engaging the Coalition's best pilots.

The diverse single-player and cooperative campaign, and the fast-paced deathmatch game, require expert piloting skills and an adept grasp on *StarLancer*'s ships and weapons. To consistently survive encounters on the Alliance-Coalition frontline and on the online battlefield, you'll need guidance that only the experts can provide.

That's where this official strategy guide comes in. Written with the full support of the Warthog, Digital Anvil, and Microsoft design teams, this *StarLancer* guide provides essential strategies to enhance your game and help defeat the enemy Coalition.

How to Use This Book

The sections that follow provide a brief overview of the chapters you'll find within the *StarLancer* official strategy guide. Be sure to study the concepts and tactics outlined in the first two sections before diving into the mission walkthroughs and multiplayer warfare sections, as success requires acute knowledge of all ship systems, maneuvers, and special abilities.

Part 1—Alliance Academy: Combat Training

Chapters 1 and 2 begin your fighter training with the fundamental skills and techniques that apply to all the ships and weapons you'll operate in *StarLancer*. You'll learn essential tactics, including the importance of an intuitive control setup, how to master standard ship equipment, and how to effectively control your wingmen. Combat training also introduces you to the fine art of dogfighting enemy fighters, bombers, and capital ships.

Chapter 1 covers concepts applicable to every *StarLancer* ship and situation. Here you'll learn the most important ship functions, including key elements of the heads-up display, how to best use your wingmen in battle, and how to adjust the power management system to suit your ship's immediate needs.

Chapter 2 shifts the focus to dogfighting. In this chapter you'll learn expert techniques regarding fighter-to-fighter dogfights along with some tips on eliminating bombers, torpedoes, and capital ships. Covered topics include how to prepare your fighter for battle, optimum attack angles, managing power systems, and avoiding primary and secondary weapons fire. Chapter 2 tactics can be applied to both single or multiplayer *StarLancer* situations, and offers some of the most important tactics in the guide.

Part 2—Alliance Intelligence: Ships and Weapons

Chapters 3 and 4 include the hardcore statistics for each of *StarLancer*'s Alliance and Coalition fighters and capital ships. You'll also find the numbers on each of *StarLancer*'s primary and secondary weapons. Strategies are included with each ship and weapon.

Chapter 3 covers the fighter arsenals of the Alliance and the Coalition. Here you'll find important statistics for each ship, including speed, agility, acceleration, and shield and armor ratings, as well as default primary weapons, missile hardpoints, afterburner quantity, and special abilities. Tactics applicable to single- and multiplayer games are also covered in detail.

Chapter 4 features the primary (guns) and secondary (missiles) weapons available to all *StarLancer* pilots. Vital battle statistics include projectile speed, rate of fire, damage potential to armor and shields, lock time, and lock distance. You'll also find descriptions and strategies for getting the most out of each weapon.

Part 3—Alliance Missions: Tour of Duty

Chapters 5 through 10 place you in the middle of the Alliance-Coalition war. This section takes you through all six campaigns of *Starlancer*'s single-player game. You'll find a complete briefing, recommended ship and missile load outs, and a detailed walkthrough covering all in-game objectives for each mission.

Part 4—Multiplayer Combat

Chapters 11 and 12 take the battle to the deathmatch and cooperative gaming arena. In this section you'll find specific *StarLancer* techniques that apply to the game's multiplayer modes of play.

Chapter 11 provides strategies for *StarLancer*'s deathmatch game, and covers specific game types and power-ups. If you're looking to shoot down your online friends and enemies with greater consistency, this section is for you. Topics include the challenges of dogfighting a human opponent, and how to use available ships, weapons, and power-ups effectively.

Chapter 12 covers *StarLancer*'s cooperative multiplayer mode. Here you'll find strategies for communicating with your fellow human pilots, selecting targets, combining your attack strengths, and techniques for specific situations.

Appendix

Appendix A reveals all of *StarLancer*'s campaign and valor medals and how to receive each. Use the appendix as a reference to stock your medal chest with the Alliance's highest honors.

In Appendix B you'll find an interview with the *StarLancer* design team. Learn the ins and outs of making an epic space combat simulator. Topics include designing missions, balancing ships and weapons, inspiration for the storyline, and how the *StarLancer* universe connects to Digital Anvil's upcoming game, *Freelancer*.

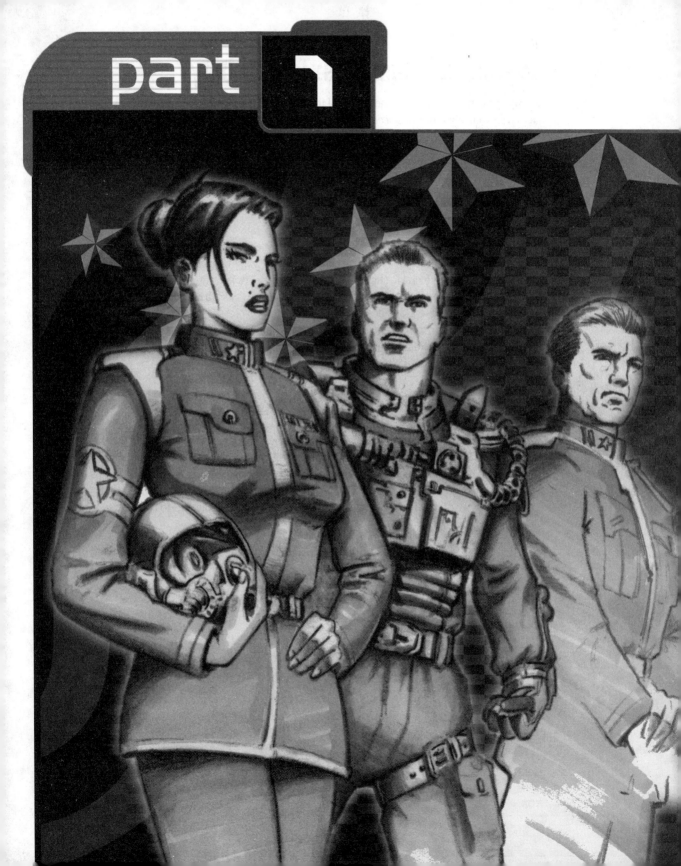

part 1

Alliance Academy:

Combat Training

Welcome to the 45th Volunteers, pilots! Before launching into battle against the Coalition, take time to study the Alliance combat training and transform yourself from an inexperienced recruit to a hardened veteran. "Part I —Alliance Academy: Combat Training" introduces you to the fundamentals of *StarLancer* fighter combat. Successful sorties in both single- and multiplayer missions require the thorough knowledge of ship systems and combat techniques outlined in these two chapters.

Chapter 1 covers the fundamentals of piloting a *StarLancer* fighter. This includes setting up an intuitive control scheme, reading your heads-up display indicators, adjusting power management, and commanding wingmen.

Chapter 2 applies the first chapter's concepts specifically to ship-to-ship dogfighting. Study this chapter for tips on preparing your ship for battle, reaching optimal attack positions, evading primary and secondary weapons fire, and assaulting bombers, torpedoes, and capital ships.

chapter 1

Flight Training

Successful ship-to-ship combat in *StarLancer* requires more than skilled dogfighting maneuvers and the largest weapon. It's often the perceptive pilot with the most knowledge about fighter basics and ship systems that emerges dominant in battle situations. Before you study the specific combat maneuvers and tactics in the next chapter, take time to grasp the fundamentals presented here.

This chapter provides essential strategies that can be applied to every flight and combat situation you'll face in *StarLancer*'s single-player campaign or multiplayer game. You'll learn the basics of fighter control, targeting, managing the power distribution system, and controlling your wingmen to your advantage.

Ship Fundamentals

Knowledge of ship characteristics and weapons won't mean anything unless you have a firm grasp on *StarLancer*'s fundamentals. The ability to quickly destroy enemy fighters, run down launched torpedoes, and assault capital ships requires both an effective control configuration and the skill to implement it in your game.

This section provides tactics for getting the most out of your ship's mobility, speed, and targeting. The most important *StarLancer* keys are described, and suggestions are given on how to apply them to your comfortable control scheme.

Mobility

StarLancer's fast-paced warfare demands lightning-quick reflexes and a complementary controller. Though you may find battle success with a keyboard or gamepad, a flight or arcade joystick (like those used in flight simulators and action games) provides the best chance to achieve consistent victories.

Mobility refers to positioning your ship's viewpoint, which in turn affects your ship's heading (in both offensive and evasive maneuvers) and targeting ability. This includes both adjusting your fighter's nose as well as rolling its body left and right. Moving your ship effectively serves as the foundation from which everything else stems. Switching directions adeptly and intuitively enables quicker kills, better evasion of missiles and turrets, and faster interception of fighter and torpedo targets.

No matter which controller you use, take the time to visit *StarLancer*'s extensive configuration screen and set up your ship's movement keys to your liking (see Figure 1.1). A comfortable pilot is a successful pilot. If you're uncomfortable positioning your ship's viewpoint, everything—accelerating, targeting, and attacking—will feel clumsy and you'll be at a significant disadvantage against the Coalition pilots in the campaign game and the human opponents online.

note

> **StarLancer fighters also include side thrusters that permit moderate strafing, or side-to-side, movement. Use the strafing thrusters for precise, controlled movements during assaults on base and capital ship subsystems. Strafe during fighter combat when trying to keep crosshairs on a target, or when dodging such things as head-on attacks.**

Speed

Speed determines your ability to reach mission objectives, eliminate enemy fighters, and protect friendly craft from torpedo and fighter attack. Though fighters will never run out of the fuel required to propel their engines to standard top speeds, your ship's afterburners, which provide a significant temporary velocity boost, are limited by a specific fuel supply. Many missions hinge on your ability to carefully manage afterburner fuel. So remember to use controlled bursts to engage enemy fighters and save the majority of your afterburner fuel for reaching and defending critical targets.

Figure 1.1: The first step in *StarLancer* dominance: tweaking the control configuration.

Maintaining your ship's speed and completing mission objectives quickly often go hand-in-hand. With several salvos of Coalition torpedoes headed at your command ship, the only way you'll intercept them all is with an acute knowledge of your ship's capabilities and knowing how to use the afterburner and matching speed ability to optimum effect.

StarLancer's ships include several important speed-related keys and abilities. The following is a rundown of each key available and how to best apply them to your game.

> **tip**
>
> Conserve afterburner fuel by diverting additional power to your ship's engines with the power distribution system, discussed later in this chapter. While you won't be able to reach your top afterburner speed, you won't waste any additional fuel. Keep in mind that both gun reserve and shield charge will be hindered by your diversion.

Accelerate (=): The accelerate key increases your ship's velocity. Apart from speed matching, you'll likely want to be at full throttle for the majority of the mission, particularly during fighter, dogfighting, and torpedo intercepting segments. Bind acceleration to your joystick's throttle, if applicable.

Decelerate (−): Decelerate decreases your ship's velocity. Like acceleration, bind decelerate to your joystick's throttle if possible. *StarLancer* fighters can accelerate and decelerate very quickly; use this to your advantage around enemy bases and capital ships to slow down and line up with critical subtargets or speed up and avoid laser turret fire.

Afterburners (Tab): Afterburners push your ship's velocity above and beyond its maximum level, even with full power diverted to the engines. Each fighter carries a particular amount of afterburner fuel, which can be increased by equipping fuel pods on the ship's missile hardpoints. The use of afterburners greatly affects a mission's outcome, especially if you're intercepting enemy craft or torpedoes, or need to reach a specific target quickly. Configure the default afterburners key to something within easy reach, as you'll use it quite often!

 Match Speed (Z): Speed matching is one of the most important elements in effective dogfighting (speed matching is discussed in more detail in Chapter 2, "Dogfighting Strategies"). With an enemy or friendly ship targeted, matching speed will automatically adjust your ship's throttle to match their velocity perfectly. This enables you to maintain your crosshairs on an enemy target much easier, as you won't overshoot the vessel or fall too far behind. Also, it's invaluable for eliminating the slower bombers and torpedoes quickly and safely (see Figure 1.2). Again, be sure to configure the default match-speed key to something easily accessible.

Figure 1.2: Speed matching enables you to safely destroy torpedo bombers without ramming into their backsides or their launched torpedoes.

 Jump Drive (J): Your ship's jump drive takes you to a mission's next Navigation point. As a general rule, don't activate your jump drive unless prompted by other wingmen or Alliance Command. Make sure all current Nav point objectives are complete before moving onward.

Targeting

An essential tool for *StarLancer* mission success, targeting allows you to pinpoint the location of enemy fighters, bombers, torpedoes, and capital ships. Once targeted, you can easily follow the opposing vessel with your ship's mobility and speed and use guns and missiles for quick elimination. Without targeting, it's difficult to strike an enemy craft with primary weapons, and impossible to launch locking missiles—with the exception of the Solomon fire-and-forget missile, a missile that locks on after launch.

The three most important features of targeting are the target direction indicator, the lead cursor, and the missile targeting ring. The target direction indicator is a small red arrow positioned around your crosshairs and indicates the direction you need to move to reestablish sight of the vessel. If you lose sight of your goal, simply move your viewpoint in the target indicator's direction.

The lead cursor is an integral part of primary weapons use. In order to hit a moving enemy effectively, you must aim your guns at the lead cursor and not at the target itself. The lead cursor considers the speed and direction of both your ship and your target and attempts to estimate an accurate firing position.

Finally, the missile targeting ring forms a white circle around your crosshairs once you're within firing range. You must maintain sight of your target for several seconds before a tone indicates that you've achieved a missile lock. For more on lock range and time, head over to Chapter 4, "Weapon Strategies and Statistics." Missiles, with the exception of the fire-and-forget Solomon and the dumb-fire Screamer, require a full lock before launch.

Blind Fire greatly enhances your ship's targeting and primary weapon abilities by automatically tracking any target within your crosshairs. Check Chapter 3, "Ship Strategies and Statistics" for a full list of *StarLancer* fighters equipped with Blind Fire and its applications in mission combat.

StarLancer uses several targeting shortcuts to enhance combat and escort situations.

Smart targeting (Ctrl+E): Toggling smart targeting enables you to automatically target any enemy vessel fired upon. It's especially useful when combating a swarm of enemy fighters, but not as helpful if you need to engage a specific vessel.

Cycle through enemies within range (E): Though you will find the targeting-the-nearest-enemy key more useful, this function locates specific targets by cycling through all enemies within range, and in the mission area.

Select primary mission target (A): Use this key should you need to quickly locate the mission objective's main target, such as a specific enemy fighter or subsystem. It's especially beneficial if you need to engage enemy fighter cover before assaulting the specific mission target. When ready, you can retarget the objective quickly without having to cycle through targets or subtargets.

Select object under reticle (Y): Operating somewhat like smart targeting, this key instantly targets the enemy or friendly craft within your crosshairs. You'll find this advantageous if you lose track of your current target and locate another. Press this key instead of cycling through a list.

Select incoming bombers and torpedoes (T): One of the most important targeting keys, this shortcut quickly targets enemy bombers and torpedoes in the mission area. Torpedo interception is difficult, but often required for mission success, so configure this key to something easily accessible. This way you can cut down on your response time to enemy bomber and torpedo presence (see Figure 1.3).

Select nearest enemy (R): Selecting the nearest enemy is particularly important during dogfighting situations where you'll want to swiftly move from one vessel to the next. Configure the select-nearest-enemy key to something close at hand to hasten your elimination of the enemy presence.

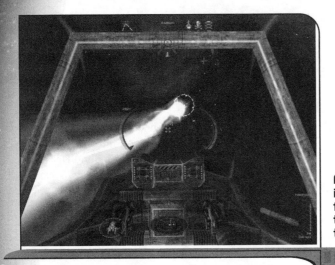

Figure 1.3: Enemy torpedoes inflict incredible damage to friendly ships. Use the shortcut to locate and target their position as quickly as possible.

 Cycle through subtargets (S): Capital ships and bases feature subtargets, such as shield generators, engines, and laser turrets. Once you've targeted the capital ship or base, use this key to cycle through its vital subsystems. Destroying the targeted subsystem will automatically advance you to the next one.

 Cycle through friendly units (Q): Use this key to cycle through friendly units and determine their damage status.

 Select nearest friendly unit (W): This key targets the nearest friendly unit so you can maintain escort or defensive position and view its damage status.

Active subtargets are highlighted red on the capital ship, or base, for easy identification. Target the capital ship or base, then cycle through to the appropriate subtarget. Approach and look for the highlighted section to pinpoint the subtarget. The targeting reticle will also surround the highlighted system.

Ship Systems

Learning about ship systems is the next important step in mastering *StarLancer*'s fierce ship-to-ship combat. Once you've grasped the fundamentals described earlier in this chapter, you're prepared to move on to your fighter's systems, each of which affects how your ship moves, targets, and performs in battle.

This section outlines *StarLancer*'s important ship systems, including power distribution, target display, and wingman communication.

Power Distribution

StarLancer's power distribution system allows you to alter your ship's speed, primary weapons, and defenses in order to get the most (or least) out of a system in a specific battle situation.

To activate the power distribution system, press the "P" key. By default, power is diverted equally among the three systems. To adjust each, simply hold down "P" while moving your joystick toward the system's icon on the power distribution display.

Although you will likely have plenty of success without ever adjusting your ship's power levels, you can make specific situations much easier to handle by tinkering with the display. Certain situations call for additional primary weapons power, a boost in speed, or better shielding. Recognize these circumstances when they develop and adjust your power levels accordingly.

StarLancer's three powered systems are outlined below along with specific situations for their use. The shortcut key to divert full power to the particular system is also included with each entry.

warning

Be careful when haphazardly diverting full power to a specific ship system, as the loss of power severely hinders the other two systems. For instance, don't forget that you've given full power to the engines in order to reach a specific target. If you do, you might neglect to readjust your power levels. As a result, your shields and guns won't recharge efficiently, making it difficult to mount an attack or defend yourself.

Guns (U): Determines how quickly the ship's primary weapons recharge. With more power diverted to the gun system, your primary weapons recharge faster. Divert more power to the guns when you're not threatened by enemies or you want to destroy an immobile target quickly. As a norm, however, you probably want to take some power away from the guns at the beginning of each mission and divert the extra energy to shields or speed. Until you run into recharge problems, don't worry about replenishing the system's power.

Shields (O): Determines how quickly the shield systems recharge after being struck by enemy guns or missiles, or by a collision. Diverting more energy to the shields enables them to recharge faster, thus protecting your hull armor from damage. Boost your shields when under attack by multiple fighters or for protection against capital ship and base laser turret defenses (see Figure 1.4). Combine additional shield strength with shield balancing (discussed in detail in Chapter 2, "Dogfighting Strategies") to improve your chances of surviving a battle unscathed.

Engines (P): Engine power sets your ship's top speed. Divert additional resources to the engines if you need to reach a target quickly and want to conserve afterburner fuel. Though you won't travel quite as fast as you would with the afterburners engaged, it's an invaluable alternative.

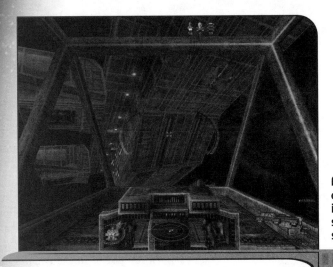

Figure 1.4: When you're this close to an enemy laser turret, it's wise to pump most of your ship's power to the shield system.

Target Display

The lower-right corner of your ship's HUD contains the target display, which is activated once you've acquired a friendly or enemy target. This display provides invaluable information on your target's speed, range, and current status. Use it to make minor adjustments in your plan of attack, including which weapons to use and how to regulate your ship's power distribution system.

Once you've targeted a friendly or enemy vessel using the methods described earlier in this chapter, you'll activate the target display and receive the following information:

 Name of target: Reveals the specific squadron to which the ship belongs, or a particular pilot that's controlling the vessel (such as an Alliance or Coalition ace pilot).

 Ship type: The type of Alliance or Coalition fighter, bomber, capital ship, cargo ship, or civilian ship.

Range: The distance from your ship to the target. Helps determine how much energy you should divert to your fighter's engines to reach the objective more quickly (or if you should toggle on the afterburners). Additionally, range helps gauge the distance you need to cover to obtain a missile lock.

 Speed: The speed of your current target. If your target eclipses your current top speed, you should divert additional power to your engine systems so you can match its speed and not fall behind.

Shield and armor status: Ship status is displayed differently on fighters and bombers than on capital ships. On fighters and bombers, the outer ring represents its shield status while the inner ring depicts hull integrity. On capital ships, a segmented bar gauge on the right side of the target display indicates its remaining hull strength. Use the enemy ship status display to gauge what's required to deliver the finishing blow. If you only need to inflict minor damage to destroy the target, consider saving missiles and use primary weapons only (see Figure 1.5). Plus, on fighters and bombers, you can see which side of the enemy craft has sustained the most damage and adjust your attack accordingly.

 Subtarget: Capital ships, bases, and other large friendly and enemy craft contain subtargets, such as shield generators, engines, and laser turrets. A segmented bar damage gauge accompanies a brief description of the subsystem.

Enemy fighters, bombers, and capital ships often change speeds during a mission. Match speed with the target so you won't have to make constant adjustments to your throttle or power distribution system. If you need a close approach, a few short, controlled bursts of the afterburner will help you reach the destination.

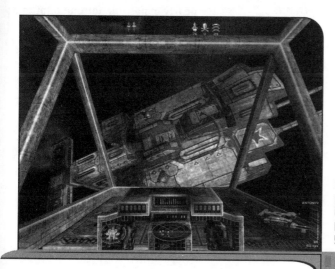

Figure 1.5: This Coalition pickup ship is within an inch of its life. Finish off the ship with primary weapons and conserve your missiles.

Communications Display

Once activated with the "C" key, the communications display appears in the upper-left corner of your ship's HUD. The gamer must navigate through several menu choices—for instance, if you wish to send a message to a specific wingman, all wingmen, an Alliance base, or an Alliance rearming ship—before issuing the specific command.

Wingman orders are outlined below along with their shortcut key. Use them carefully during combat situations; effective use of wingmen can turn a difficult mission into a manageable one.

 "Attack My Target" (F5): Orders specific wingmen (or all wingmen) to engage specific targets to hasten their destruction. This is especially effective on smaller capital ships, such as the Coalition

Kurgens, and useful if you need specific attacking fighters destroyed before they reach critical friendly targets. Don't order your wingmen to attack a target too powerful for them to destroy or you'll likely hear them ejecting from their exploded vessels one by one. Keep them engaged with Coalition fighters before tackling the mission's tougher adversaries.

"Back Off" (F6): This is very useful in conjunction with the wing status display (activated with the "X" key). If you see specific wingmen taking too much damage while attacking a target, order them to back off. Keeping wingmen healthy for the entire mission makes the last, and usually more difficult, segments much easier.

"Help Me" (F7): If you're engaged with multiple targets and need assistance, radio a wingman with this command. The wingman will then target the enemy craft assaulting your vessel. With the enemy diverted and engaged, you can resume your dogfighting, torpedo interception, or capital ship assault duties.

If Coalition bombers enter the mission area and target friendly craft with launched torpedoes, order your wingmen to destroy the bomber while you take out the torpedoes. It's nearly impossible for one pilot to do both, but ordering wingmen against the bomber should mean fewer torpedoes to deal with.

chapter 2
Dogfighting Strategies

Consistent *StarLancer* success hinges on your ability to apply the fundamentals and knowledge of ship systems gained from Chapter 1 in battle situations. Whether you're ordered to patrol a navigation point, assault a Coalition base, or defend an Alliance convoy from attack, you'll encounter ship-to-ship dogfighting in each *StarLancer* mission.

Before heading out into the dangerous single-player campaign or multiplayer arena, study the combat concepts outlined in this chapter. Over the following pages you'll learn everything there is to know about preparing your ship for fighter combat, reaching the optimum attack angles, missile evasion, torpedo and bomber interception, and assaulting heavily-armed capital ships.

Combat Readiness

Mission success doesn't always start with the fighter-to-fighter encounter; it often begins back in the mission briefing! Though it's important to study the ship maneuvers and weapon techniques required to eliminate enemy vessels with consistency, it's equally crucial to remember certain combat concepts that apply to every battle situation.

In this section you'll discover the importance of selecting a ship and load out to complement the mission objectives, remaining aware of your mission surroundings, discerning targeting decisions, and preparing for an imminent combat situation.

Briefing Decisions

Listen carefully during *StarLancer*'s campaign mission briefings and make decisions about your ship selection and missile load out accordingly. For instance, if you're escorting an Alliance convoy through Coalition space, you can expect an attack that will usually involve torpedoes. To best fend them off, choose a swift ship with high speed, acceleration, and agility ratings. Torpedo interception relies more on top speed and afterburner fuel than it does on shield power and hull integrity (see Figure 2.1).

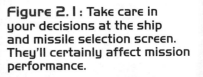

Figure 2.1: Take care in your decisions at the ship and missile selection screen. They'll certainly affect mission performance.

Conversely, missions that include assaults on Coalition bases or capital ships require an Alliance fighter with superior firepower and durability. You wouldn't want to pilot a flimsy fighter around a capital ship's powerful laser turrets. For more on ship characteristics and strategies, head to Chapter 3, "Ship Strategies and Statistics."

Mission selection works similarly. If you're escorting or protecting Alliance craft, you're certain to face Coalition fighters and bombers. If this is the case, then select a number of powerful locking missiles. If you're sent out against Coalition capital ships or an enemy base, you should select dumb-fire or several slow, but powerful, Jackhammer missiles. Check out Chapter 4, "Weapon Strategies and Statistics" for a detailed look at all of *StarLancer*'s weaponry.

Mission Awareness

Upon entering a new mission area or navigation point, cycle through available friendly and enemy targets and examine their current speed and distance from your position. Then activate your offensive and defensive systems accordingly. Also, be aware of the situation going into a new navigation point. Be prepared to immediately engage Coalition forces, use your afterburner to quickly reach a critical friendly target, or perform whatever task your current mission objective demands.

The necessity of mission awareness continues well into the actual battle. For instance, remain cognizant of your location in relation to enemy craft, particularly capital ships. If you're engaged with several Coalition fighters, don't stray too close to a Coalition capital ship—you'll likely take unnecessary shield and armor damage from the larger vessel's laser turrets. On the other hand, if you're called to protect an Alliance vessel from attack, don't stray too far to combat individual fighters. Stay relatively close to the ship you're guarding and engage the attackers, or torpedoes, as they approach.

Target Selection

Once you're embroiled in a tense combat situation, it's important to be selective about your targets. Assess the mission area's greatest threats and adjust your battle plan accordingly. For example, if Alliance Command announces the presence of Coalition bombers while you're occupied with fighters, disengage from the dogfight and engage the bombers (see Figure 2.2).

It's also vital to assess the damage of any current enemy targets. If you've pummeled an opponent to near destruction, consider advancing to the next craft, especially if you're attempting to protect friendly ships from primary and secondary weapon fire. Order your wingmen against the weakened fighter while you move on to the bigger threats. You won't get the credit for the kill, but you'll likely improve your chances for mission success.

tip

Remember to ask questions after failing a mission. What went wrong? Was your ship not strong enough to withstand the Coalition forces? Was your fighter too slow to intercept the enemy vessels and torpedoes? Replay the mission only after coming up with some answers and adjusting your ship and/or load out accordingly.

tip

Watch your communication display and listen to your fellow wingmen during battle situations. A wingman often sends an alert if you're under attack from a Coalition fighter or threatened by an enemy missile. Don't tune out your allies or you'll suffer serious consequences.

Figure 2.2: Enemy bombers always pose a significant threat to friendly capital ships, so make them a priority!

Battle Preparation

Ship-to-ship combat dominates *StarLancer*'s single- and multiplayer games. Every aspect centers on your engagement with Coalition fighters, bombers, capital ships, or fellow human pilots in multiplayer games online. Though crafty maneuvers and well-placed primary and secondary weapons eventually deliver killing blows, the steps you take before the engagement can have a significant impact on battle success or failure.

As you approach each enemy target, make the following preparations to your fighter.

 Replenish and rebalance shields: If you've suffered shield damage from a prior encounter, quickly divert the majority of your ship's power to the shield system to recharge quickly. You should also use the shield-balance key (defaults to the "N" key) to adjust shields over your entire hull. Once they're replenished, restore power to your ship's gun and engine systems.

 Target the nearest threat: Use the targeting shortcuts to lock on to the nearest fighter, bomber, or torpedo. Adjust your ship's heading on an intercept course to the target. Depending on the distance, you may need to increase your engine power or toggle on the ship's afterburners.

Prepare the power distribution system: Adjust your ship's power distribution system according to the identity of your next target. If you're up against fighters, divert more power to guns and shields and less to engines, especially if you can outrun them or have plenty of afterburner fuel. If you're engaging bombers and torpedoes, shift power to the engines and neglect shields and guns for the time being. If you're assaulting capital ships, divert more power to shields, an additional sum to guns, and less to engines.

Shift shield strength: Hold down the shield-balancing key and use your controller to shift shield strength to either the forward or rear shields. If you're assaulting capital ships, move shield strength forward to protect yourself from the laser turrets you'll face. If you're intercepting torpedoes, shift shield strength backward to protect your rear hull against any pursuing fighters.

Set primary weapons to full guns: If you're piloting a fighter equipped with more than one primary weapon, set them to "full guns" for greater damage potential. You can also synchronize them so that all projectiles fire at once.

Ready your secondary weapons: Cycle through your equipped secondary weapons and, depending on the current target, prepare your most useful missile. If you're approaching a swarm of fighters, prepare Havoc, Imp, or Solomon missiles. Should you engage bombers or torpedoes, prepare locking missiles like the Raptor or Hawk. If you're up against a capital ship, ready Jackhammers or Screamers.

Activate your afterburner: Toggle on your ship's afterburner should you need to reach a friendly or enemy target quickly and full engine power just isn't fast enough. Equip additional fuel pods at the missile load out screen if you've selected a ship with a small afterburner supply.

Activate your fighter's Blind Fire or Spectral Shields ability: If you selected a fighter with Blind Fire or Spectral Shields, prepare their use as you approach targets. Blind Fire assists in the destruction of fighters and torpedoes, while Spectral Shields provides temporary invincibility against enemy fire. The latter is particularly useful when near an enemy capital ship's powerful laser turrets (see Figure 2.3).

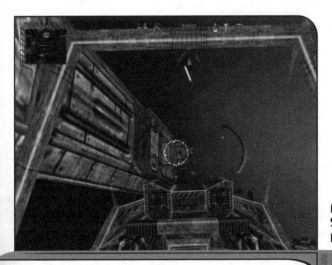

Figure 2.3: Switch on Spectral Shields if you're in close proximity to capital ship turrets.

Prepare ship's electronic countermeasures for use: Shields and hull armor won't last long if you're flying close to an enemy base or capital ship's laser turrets. To provide extra defense against these weapons, prepare your ship's electronic countermeasures (ECM) for use. Each ship carries a varying amount of ECM energy. Check Chapter 3, "Ship Strategies and Statistics" for a complete list of ships and their corresponding ECM duration.

 Prepare countermeasures for use: Countermeasures, or decoys, help protect your ship against enemy missiles. When you're about to engage enemy fighters, ready your countermeasure key in case your enemy locks on with secondary weapons. Like ECM energy, each ship carries a different number of countermeasures. For the complete list, head into Chapter 3, "Ship Strategies and Statistics."

Engage target with primary and secondary weapons: The final step in battle preparation is the battle itself. The remaining sections in this chapter detail battle tactics for each combat situation.

Combat Tactics

Decisions made during the ship and missile selection and your preparations made upon entering the mission area all converge at *StarLancer*'s most important element: ship-to-ship combat with the enemy. Hesitation often creates a more difficult situation. You must become adept at ship fundamentals, systems, and selection, as well as battle preparation, in order to survive the increasingly difficult combat missions.

This section provides tactics for engaging enemy fighters, intercepting bombers and torpedoes, and assaulting capital ships and their subtargets.

Engaging Fighters

To prevent retaliation with primary and secondary weapons, attack enemy fighters from the rear. After targeting the enemy craft, use your target direction indicator—the red arrow positioned around your crosshairs—to pinpoint its location. Then adjust your heading to match that of your target.

If you approach the fighter head-on, shift shield strength forward to protect your hull. When you pass it, use the direction indicator once again to follow the enemy fighter. If you approach it from the rear—the desired position since you're out of the enemy's line of fire—ready primary and secondary weapons for use (see Figure 2.4).

Reaching your enemy's rear position isn't the difficult part; it's maintaining that position on your target. As you pursue, the opponent will make every effort to shake your crosshairs loose.

tip

If your target's top speed eclipses your own, adjust your ship's power distribution system by diverting additional power to the engines. You can also use short bursts of afterburner to compensate for the speed difference.

Figure 2.4: Engaging fighters from behind keeps your ship safe from significant damage.

Preserve your attack position on the target by matching its attitude and direction by rotating or changing your ship's pitch and direction.

Matching speed is the most important way to maintain your attack position. With your speed matched, you won't need to worry about overrunning or falling behind your target. You'll remain the same distance from the enemy craft by following its maneuvers using the target directional indicator.

As you pursue, maintain the enemy in your crosshairs to establish a missile lock. Once you've achieved this, launch secondary weapons. Line up your crosshair with the lead cursor positioned around the target's reticle (which automatically adjusts depending on speed and heading) to fire accurate primary weapon shots.

Once you've destroyed the enemy fighter, press the target-nearest-enemy button (or cycle through the available targets), engage the next enemy ship, and repeat the entire process.

Evading Missiles

Every *StarLancer* battle situation consists of give and take. Sometimes you'll be on the attack, while moments later you'll be on the defensive. Enemy fighters constantly look for opportunities to swoop down on you from behind or launch locking missiles at your fighter.

note

Missiles are deceived by countermeasures. For a complete list of missiles, and their susceptibility to decoys, head over to Chapter 4, "Weapon Strategies and Statistics."

Deploy your ship's countermeasures to escape locked missiles. Often, a wingman will announce when an enemy missile has locked onto your ship. Also, look for the missile threat indicator—positioned above your crosshairs—which alerts you to an enemy locked missile.

Be sure to control your deployment of countermeasures. Keep an eye on the missile threat indicator. If it remains lit after countermeasures have been used, then the missile remains locked on to your ship. Continue to release countermeasures one at a time until you've fooled the incoming missile. Copious use of the afterburner and sharp shifts in direction also help buy your ship extra time to either evade or fool the missile with the decoys.

Escaping from Multiple Fighters

Another threat indicator positioned above your crosshairs alerts you if your ship is under primary weapons attack from one or more enemy fighters (your wingmen also often announce that you're in danger). Consistent pounding from primary weapons often depletes shield strength faster than missiles, so don't ignore warnings that you're under attack. Peel off your current target by applying additional throttle or by using your ship's afterburner. Switch directions and attempt to engage the fighter, or fighters, attacking your craft. If you're overwhelmed, toggle on the afterburner and retreat while you order wingmen to attack the targets and help you out (see Figure 2.5).

Figure 2.5: Activate your afterburner to retreat from dangerous situations.

Should you suffer damage to your ship's shields or hull, divert additional power to shields and offset the decreased top speed by using afterburner fuel to escape. Use the shield-balancing key to restore any damaged shields or to shift strength to the front or rear, depending on the location of your attackers.

Intercepting Torpedoes and Bombers

Protecting critical friendly convoy and capital ships from torpedo attack takes a controlled mix of speed, mobility, and target selection. During *StarLancer*'s campaign, listen to your communications carefully; Allied Command or wingmen will always announce the arrival of Coalition torpedo bombers, as these will require your immediate attention.

Don't cycle through all enemy targets to locate bombers or torpedoes. Always use the target-nearest-torpedo shortcut (which also cycles through bombers in the mission area) to pinpoint the location of enemy warheads. Seek out and engage the closest torpedo or bomber threat.

Bombers are durable, but sluggish. Because torpedoes are the only threat to friendly craft, don't waste too much time in eliminating the vessels themselves. Ready locking missiles, and fire two or three at the bomber's hull. Screamers also prove effective, as the virtually immobile enemy provides an easy target for the dumb fire missiles.

Torpedo interception often requires valuable afterburner fuel and the selection of a speedy ship after the mission briefing. Equip extra fuel pods if the briefing calls for escort or ship protection. If this isn't possible, divert additional power to your ship's engines to increase top speed. Torpedoes can be eliminated with locking missiles from a distance or with primary weapons as you approach. Match the torpedo's speed as you near it in order to prevent over-running or ramming into the warhead—a miscue that will instantly destroy your ship.

tip

Coalition bombers jump out of the mission area once they've launched their entire payload. Concentrate on destroying the torpedoes. If you make a run for the bomber itself, some warheads might slip by and reach their Alliance target.

Eliminating Capital Ships and Base Subsystems

Approach enemy capital ships and bases with defense systems activated. Be sure to divert additional power to shields, shift shield strength forward, activate ECM, and enable Spectral Shields as laser turrets can rip apart a fighter's shields and hull armor in only a few shots. Preparing your ship before you come within the turrets' firing range is your only real defense.

A fighter's relatively weak primary and secondary weapons can't penetrate the durable shields and hull armor of a capital ship or base. Instead, you must inflict damage by destroying the ship or base's sub-targets, which could include engines, shield generators, laser turrets, or other specialized sections. Target the ship or base and cycle through its subtargets with the shortcut key. Targeted subsystems are highlighted in red, distinguishing them from the rest of the enemy. Approach from an unobstructed angle and eliminate the subsystem with primary or secondary weapons (see Figure 2.6).

When maneuvering around capital ship or base laser turrets, maintain a balance between decreasing speed and increasing durability. Decreasing your speed—almost to a stop—will unleash a constant stream of primary weapons fire, allowing you to quickly eliminate any subtargets. If you remain at standard speed levels, it

tip

Outfit your ship with Jackhammer missiles if the briefing calls for capital ship or base assault. The powerful Alliance warhead can destroy most systems in a single blow. Before you fire, make sure the subtarget isn't obstructed by other sections of the ship or base. One Jackhammer occupies one hardpoint, so you can't afford to waste them!

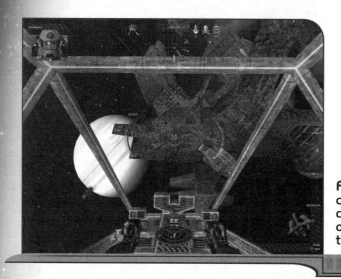

Figure 2.6: When attacking a capital ship subsystem, make certain your line of fire isn't obstructed by other sections of the vessel.

will likely take several passes to destroy the subtarget. Please note that at a decreased speed you'll be an easier target for the laser turrets; so you must keep shields balanced and replenished by diverting engine power (which you're not using) to the shield system.

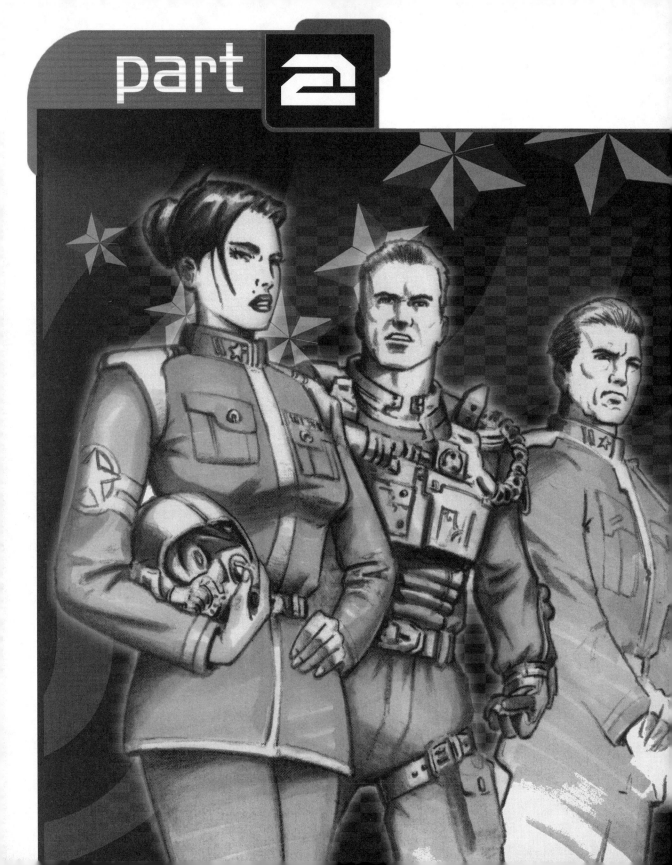

part 2

Alliance Intelligence:

Ships and Weapons

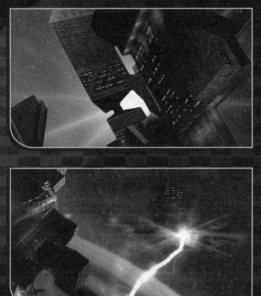

In "Part 2—Alliance Intelligence: Ships and Weapons" you'll find data for all of *StarLancer*'s fighters and weapons, along with tactics for applying each to the single- and multiplayer games.

Chapter 3 features detailed statistics for all Alliance and Coalition fighters. Key statistics covered include speed, agility, acceleration, shield, and armor ratings, default primary weaponry, missile hardpoints, afterburner fuel, ECM (Electronic Counter-Measures) time, countermeasures, and special abilities. Strategies for using each playable Alliance fighter and defeating each Coalition enemy are also offered. A chart at the end of the chapter includes stats for bombers, as well as cargo, pickup, and capital ships.

Chapter 4 delves into the statistics for Alliance primary and secondary weapons. Here you'll find projectile speeds, damage potentials, rates of fire, lock times, and other key statistics for all guns and missiles.

chapter 3

Ship Strategies and Statistics

Having completed flight and dogfight training, you're prepared to test drive a fighter of your own. *StarLancer* includes twelve different playable Alliance fighters, each with carefully balanced speed, durability, and firepower ratings. Each performs best in specific situations. Knowledge of each craft's strengths and weaknesses will provide the edge you need during hectic battle situations.

You'll find an in-depth analysis of all Alliance and Coalition fighters in this chapter. A detailed list of statistics, including speed, acceleration, agility, shield, and armor rating, as well as default afterburner, ECM, missile hardpoints, and primary weapon load outs, are included for each fighter as well. Studying the strategies contained in this chapter will help you make sound decisions and get the most out of your ships during single- and multiplayer games.

Ship Statistics Explained

The fighters discussed in this chapter are separated into Alliance and Coalition craft. The table accompanying each fighter description offers a series of relevant statistics. Below is an explanation of the terms used in the tables:

 Type: The type of ship determined by its size and statistics.

 Speed Rating: Based on a scale from one to ten, the relative speed of the ship, with higher numbers meaning faster.

 Shield Rating: Based on a scale from one to ten, the relative shield strength of the ship, with higher meaning stronger shields.

 Agility Rating: Based on a scale from one to ten, the relative maneuverability of the ship, with higher meaning more agile.

 Acceleration Rating: Based on a scale from one to ten, the relative acceleration of the ship, with higher indicating quicker acceleration.

 Gun Energy: The default amount of gun energy.

 Clearance: Clearance level or rank required to pilot the ship.

 ECM: The default amount of ECM time.

 Afterburner Fuel: The default amount of afterburner fuel.

 Decoys: The number of countermeasures loaded by default.

 Missile Hardpoints: The default number of available missile hardpoints on the ship.

 Gun Recharge: Relative speed in which the ship's guns recharge, with the higher number indicating a faster recharge.

 Displacement: Approximate weight of the ship, which affects its maneuverability.

Armor Class: Based on a scale from one to ten, the relative armor strength of the ship, with higher indicating a stronger hull.

Max Speed: Maximum speed of the fighter based on a default power distribution.

Special Features: Any special abilities equipped on the ship.

Shield Recharge: The relative speed in which the ship's shields recharge, with higher indicating a faster recharge.

Primary Weapons: The default primary weapons outfitted.

Alliance Fighters

The Alliance fighter fleet strikes a finely tuned balance between speed, maneuverability, durability, and firepower. The pilot should make careful decisions during the pre-mission briefing and select the best available ship for the task at hand. This section examines all Alliance fighters and reveals the tactics required for consistent success.

Upon starting the *StarLancer* campaign game, you only have access to four fighters—the Crusader, Grendel, Naginata, and Predator. Your choices won't expand until you prove yourself by scoring kills or completing missions.

Collecting mission kills is one way to release additional fighters for use. Making every attempt to escalate your kill score in the early missions will make future missions easier because you'll have access to additional—and usually more powerful—fighters. Concentrate on scoring as many kills as possible in the early, less dangerous, missions. If you can handle the current number of enemies on your own, consider pulling your wingmen off their targets so you're the one to score the kills.

Table 3.1 provides a reference for how kill scores are related to ship access.

Table 3.1: Ship Release Schedule – Based on Kills

Rank	Kills	Ships Released
2nd Lieutenant	0	Crusader, Grendel, Naginata, Predator
1st Lieutenant	35	Coyote
Flight Lieutenant	72	Mirage
Captain	115	Tempest
Flight Captain	150	Patriot
Lieutenant Commander	200	Wolverine
Commander	255	Reaper
Flight Commander	275	Phoenix
Squadron Commander	300	Shroud

Alliance fighters are also released after completing certain milestone missions that make up the separate campaigns. If you aren't as adept with kills, simply advancing through the single-player campaign will provide access to the new and more powerful Alliance ships.

Table 3.2 illustrates the completed missions requirement for the release of specific Alliance ships. If you haven't reached the kill score associated with the specific vessel, you'll immediately gain access to it once you complete the designated mission.

Level	Release Point	Ships
Bronze	Game Start	Crusader, Grendel, Naginata, Predator
Silver	Start Mission 12	Coyote, Mirage, Tempest
Gold	Start Mission 17	Patriot, Reaper, Wolverine
Platinum	Start Mission 19	Phoenix, Shroud

Coyote

Accessed by either scoring 35 kills or reaching Mission 12, the Alliance's Coyote fighter is one of the most versatile vessels that can be obtained in *StarLancer*'s early missions. The Coyote's durable shields and adequate armor class complement its above-average speed, agility, and excellent acceleration ratings. The medium fighter's main weakness is its lack of primary weapons power. Though it's equipped with the Blind Fire ability, the Coyote features only two Proton Cannons and a low gun recharge rate.

tip

Offset the Coyote's poor gun recharge rate with the power distribution system. Divert some energy from the shield and engine systems to the guns and increase the Coyote's primary weapons recharge.

The Coyote's Blind Fire ability makes it a top choice for torpedo interception, patrol, and escort missions. When active, Blind Fire automatically leads targeted ships within the crosshairs, making it easier to track down torpedoes and enemy fighters. Once you've released the Coyote, it's unlikely that you would need to fly the Predator or Naginata again.

Type: Medium Fighter	Clearance: 1st Lieutenant
Displacement: 3 tons	Speed Rating: 6
ECM: 20 secs.	Armor Class: 5
Shield Rating: 5	Afterburner Fuel: 100 secs.
Max Speed: 300.00	Agility Rating: 6
Decoys: 16	Special Features: Blind Fire
Acceleration Rating: 10	Missile Hardpoints: 7
Shield Recharge: 10	Gun Energy: 100.00
Gun Recharge: 5.00	Primary Weapons: 2 Proton Cannons, Rear Laser Cannon

Crusader

Offered at the start of the campaign, the Crusader provides adequate speed and decent durability. It's effective in earlier missions that call for heavy firepower and assaults on Coalition capital ships. Though it lacks the missile hardpoints of other ships (particularly the less maneuverable, but more durable and faster, Grendel), the Crusader's Spectral Shields provide limited invulnerability. This is an excellent feature when faced against the powerful laser turrets of a cruiser or Kurgen corvette.

Consider the Crusader when you need added primary weaponry and strength coupled with the ability to keep up with most Coalition fighters. Though you should select the Coyote or Predator for dogfights early in the game, the Crusader's primary weapons provide extra firepower and the Spectral Shields provide extra protection against enemy forces.

Type: Light Fighter	Clearance: 2nd Lieutenant	Displacement: 2.3 tons
Speed Rating: 5	ECM: 20 secs.	Armor Class: 5
Shield Rating: 4	Afterburner Fuel: 110 secs.	Max Speed: 260.00
Agility Rating: 6	Decoys: 12	Special Features: Spectral Shields
Acceleration Rating: 7	Missile Hardpoints: 5	Shield Recharge: 10
Gun Energy: 150.00	Gun Recharge: 8.00	Primary Weapons: 2 Gatling Lasers, Rear Laser Cannon

Grendel

Similar to the Crusader, the Grendel also proves extremely effective on Coalition capital ship assault runs. Its powerful primary weapons, plentiful missile hardpoints, and superb armor class make for an Alliance fighter with the durability to withstand the laser turrets of a capital ship and the firepower to blast through that same vessel's subsystems and armor quickly.

tip

The Grendel carries the lowest amount of afterburner fuel in the Alliance fighter fleet. If you believe the upcoming mission will require additional afterburner use, consider equipping one of the Grendel's plentiful missile hardpoints with a fuel pod.

The Grendel's weakness lies in its lack of ability to combat waves of Coalition fighters (particularly agile ones such as the Lagg and Sabre). If you expect dogfights in your capital ship assaults, but still require adequate armor and shield strength, select the Crusader or the Tempest. Leave the torpedo interception, patrol, and escort missions to the more agile Alliance fighters, as the Grendel lacks the top speed and afterburner fuel to keep up with Coalition fighters and launched torpedoes.

Type: Medium Fighter	**Clearance:** 2nd Lieutenant	**Displacement:** 4.5 tons
Speed Rating: 5	**ECM:** 20 secs.	**Armor Class:** 6
Shield Rating: 6	**Afterburner Fuel:** 80 secs.	**Max Speed:** 260.00
Agility Rating: 3	**Decoys:** 18	**Special Features:** None
Acceleration Rating: 10	**Missile Hardpoints:** 7	**Shield Recharge:** 10
Gun Energy: 90.00	**Gun Recharge:** 9.00	**Primary Weapons:** 2 Gatling Plasma Cannons, Twin Laser Cannon, Rear Laser Turret

Mirage IV

Offered upon reaching 72 kills or Mission 12, the Mirage boasts an impressive mix of speed and primary weapons firepower. This makes it an excellent dogfighting ship for pilots who prefer guns over missiles. The Mirage's ample gun energy and high recharge rate help keep its primary weapons cooled (though the Neutron Particle Gun sucks power fast). This is a good thing considering the medium fighter only comes equipped with four missile hardpoints.

Even without the secondary weapons, it's hard to pass up the Mirage for its impressive handling and gun power. For torpedo interception, patrol, and escort missions, a pilot could have a tough choice between the Mirage and the Coyote (which will also be available before or at the moment the Mirage is released). The Coyote features better armor, missile hardpoints, and the Blind Fire ability, but lacks the primary weapon firepower of its heavier cousin.

Type: Medium Fighter	Clearance: Flight Lieutenant	Displacement: 1.9 tons
Speed Rating: 7	ECM: 20 secs.	Armor Class: 4
Shield Rating: 5	Afterburner Fuel: 110 secs.	Max Speed: 320.00
Agility Rating: 6	Decoys: 14	Special Features: None
Acceleration Rating: 5	Missile Hardpoints: 4	Shield Recharge: 10
Gun Energy: 220.00	Gun Recharge: 9.00	Primary Weapons: 2 Messon Blasters, Neutron Particle Gun

Naginata

Speed and maneuverability aren't the problem of the Naginata, a light fighter available from the beginning of *StarLancer*'s campaign. Unfortunately, its durability, missile payload, and primary weapon firepower are. Though the Naginata comes equipped with Spectral Shields, providing temporary invulnerability in tense situations, select the Naginata primarily for speed-related missions such as torpedo interception and time-intensive fighter encounters. But if you have trouble staying alive, the Naginata's Spectral Shields could provide the defense you need to complete the mission with success.

The Naginata's armor class also presents a significant disadvantage in combat situations. Divert additional power from the engines or guns to the shields, as you'll need to keep them charged in order to protect the vessel's weak hull. If you're picking between the Predator and Naginata in a dogfight situation, take the Predator with its better hull strength, better acceleration, and Blind Fire feature, an excellent tool in knocking out fighters quickly.

Type: Light Fighter	Clearance: 2nd Lieutenant	Displacement: 1.5 tons
Speed Rating: 7	ECM: 20 secs.	Armor Class: 2
Shield Rating: 5	Afterburner Fuel: 130 secs.	Max Speed: 340.00
Agility Rating: 8	Decoys: 15	Special Features: Spectral Shields
Acceleration Rating: 3	Missile Hardpoints: 3	Shield Recharge: 10
Gun Energy: 180.00 Cannons	Gun Recharge: 7.00	Primary Weapons: 2 Pulse

Patriot

Available after either scoring 150 kills or reaching Mission 17, the Patriot should immediately become your primary escort and torpedo interception fighter. Though it lacks the armor rating of its Reaper and Wolverine cousins, the Patriot's excellent top speed, powerful primary weapons, and Blind Fire special ability create a potent dogfighter and interceptor.

The Patriot's main weakness is its low armor class in comparison with other medium fighters. If you're in a dog-fight situation and need shield strength and armor class over speed and gun recharge rate, use the power distribution to divert energy to the shield system. Should you be called on to mount capital ship assaults, select the more durable Wolverine, which can also hold more missiles.

Type: Medium Fighter	**Clearance:** Flight Captain	**Displacement:** 3.2 tons
Speed Rating: 7	**ECM:** 20 secs.	**Armor Class:** 5
Shield Rating: 6	**Afterburner Fuel:** 110 secs.	**Max Speed:** 340.00
Agility Rating: 4	**Decoys:** 18	**Special Features:** Blind Fire
Acceleration Rating: 10	**Missile Hardpoints:** 5	**Shield Recharge:** 10
Gun Energy: 160.00	**Gun Recharge:** 7.00	**Primary Weapons:** 2 Tachyon Cannons, 2 Proton Cannons, Rear Laser Cannon

Phoenix

Released at 275 kills or reaching Mission 19, the Phoenix is arguably the most rounded fighter in the Alliance fleet. With impressive speed that's eclipsed only by the Shroud, it performs well in escort, interception, and fighter patrol missions. Ample afterburner fuel means you shouldn't need an extra fuel pod. This is a good thing, too, since the Phoenix lacks the missile hardpoint quantity of other fighters.

Perhaps the Patriot's most unique feature is the inclusion of three special abilities: the gun-assisting Blind Fire, quick-stop Reverse Thrust, and the impressive Nova Cannon. Use the Reverse Thrust to retreat quickly from capital ships or to shake a fighter off your tail. The Nova Cannon, a recharging, single-shot devastator, should be saved for pesky fighters, Kurgens, or capital ship subtargets.

tip

If you're a pilot who relies more on missiles than guns, then you should opt for the Reaper. Though not quite as quick as the Phoenix, its ample missile hardpoints make up for its lack of velocity.

Type: Prototype Medium Fighter	Clearance: Flight Commander	Displacement: 4.6 tons
Speed Rating: 9	ECM: 20 secs.	Armor Class: 4
Shield Rating: 6	Afterburner Fuel: 140 secs.	Max Speed: 380.00
Agility Rating: 8	Decoys: 16	Special Features: Blind Fire, Reverse Thrust, Nova Cannon
Acceleration Rating: 10	Missile Hardpoints: 4	Shield Recharge: 10
Gun Energy: 180.00	Gun Recharge: 6.00	Primary Weapons: 2 Gatling Lasers, 2 Pulse Cannons, Rear Laser Turret

Predator

Offered from the start of *StarLancer*'s campaign, the Predator closely resembles the Naginata in providing competent bomber interception with moderate dogfighting ability. In a choice between the Naginata and the Predator, you should select the Naginata if you require Spectral Shields to survive a particular encounter and choose the Predator for more dogfight-intensive and torpedo-filled missions.

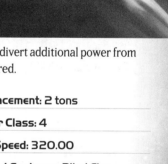

Though it carries a solid number of missile hardpoints, the Predator's primary weapons, gun energy, and gun recharge rate aren't very impressive. The Blind Fire ability, though, will help offset the ship's primary weapon shortcomings. You may wish to divert additional power from the engines to the guns or shields when speed isn't immediately required.

Type: Light Fighter	Clearance: 2nd Lieutenant	Displacement: 2 tons
Speed Rating: 7	ECM: 20 secs.	Armor Class: 4
Shield Rating: 3	Afterburner Fuel: 100 secs.	Max Speed: 320.00
Agility Rating: 8	Decoys: 10	Special Features: Blind Fire
Acceleration Rating: 6	Missile Hardpoints: 6	Shield Recharge: 10
Gun Energy: 90.00	Gun Recharge: 6.00	Primary Weapons: 2 Proton Cannons, Rear Laser Cannon

Reaper

Along with the Coyote, the Reaper is one of the best all-purpose fighters in *StarLancer*. Released after 255 kills or by making it to Mission 17, the Reaper has plentiful missile hardpoints and boasts a solid balance of speed, maneuverability, and durability. Powerful primary weapons and the Blind Fire ability make the ship an efficient dogfighting machine, while the shield rating, armor class, and missiles make it effective at assaulting capital ships.

All of these advantages make the Reaper an excellent choice once the ship is available. Its one minor downside—poor gun energy and recharge rate—can be offset with crafty use of the power distribution system. If you're in an intense dogfight and already faster than your prey, consider diverting power from engines and shields to the gun system so you're never out of primary weapon juice.

Type: Heavy Fighter	**Clearance:** Commander	**Displacement:** 4.4 tons
Speed Rating: 6	**ECM:** 20 secs.	**Armor Class:** 5
Shield Rating: 6	**Afterburner Fuel:** 120 secs.	**Max Speed:** 300.00
Agility Rating: 4	**Decoys:** 24	**Special Features:** Blind Fire
Acceleration Rating: 5	**Missile Hardpoints:** 8	**Shield Recharge:** 10
Gun Energy: 100.00	**Gun Recharge:** 7.00	**Primary Weapons:** 2 Gatling Lasers, 2 Laser Cannons, Rear Quad Pulse Turret

Shroud

An excellent interceptor and the fastest fighter in the Alliance fleet, the Shroud is released by either achieving 300 kills or reaching Mission 19. The vessel features incredible speed, maneuverability, and afterburner ratings, although its poor armor class and lack of weaponry can pose problems in combat situations.

note

One *StarLancer* campaign mission requires the selection of the Shroud. Its poor armor class comes into play during this sortie as you're called to assault a base's laser turrets. To offset the Shroud's primary weakness—its hull—divert additional power from the engines to the shields to keep the recharge rate high.

Don't dismiss the Shroud completely, though. It features four special devices—Blind Fire, Reverse Thrust, Spectral Shields, and the unique Stealth cloaking ability—creating a diverse ship that is effective in a variety of situations. Don't underestimate its Stealth cloak. Use it to avoid fighter cover and complete capital ship assault missions. Remember, however, that firing primary or secondary weapons deactivates the cloaking device.

Type: Prototype Light Fighter	**Clearance:** Squadron Commander	**Displacement:** 1.6 tons
Speed Rating: 10	**ECM:** 20 secs.	**Armor Class:** 3
Shield Rating: 7	**Afterburner Fuel:** 150 secs.	**Max Speed:** 400.00
Agility Rating: 10	**Decoys:** 10	**Special Features:** Stealth, Blind Fire, Spectral Shields, Reverse Thrust
Acceleration Rating: 3	**Missile Hardpoints:** 4	**Shield Recharge:** 10
Gun Energy: 140.00	**Gun Recharge:** 6.00	**Primary Weapons:** 2 Proton Cannons

Tempest

Released relatively early—after 115 kills or reaching Mission 12—the Tempest becomes your primary capital ship assault fighter during the middle section of *StarLancer*'s campaign. With Spectral Shields providing temporary invincibility, powerful primary weapons, ample missile hardpoints, and plentiful ECM time, the Tempest can withstand the punishment of a Coalition capital ship or corvette, but doesn't quite have the speed or decoy ability to survive hectic dogfights.

The Tempest's Tachyon Cannons consume a huge amount of gun energy during each use. With a relatively low reserve and recharge time, you'll likely need to divert power from another ship system to the guns to keep primary weapons active. With an already high shield rating and the Spectral Shields ability, consider pulling energy from shields.

Type: Heavy Fighter	Clearance: Captain	Displacement: 8 tons
Speed Rating: 6	ECM: 20 secs.	Armor Class: 5
Shield Rating: 6	Afterburner Fuel: 100 secs.	Max Speed: 300.00
Agility Rating: 4	Decoys: 12	Special Features: Spectral Shields
Acceleration Rating: 10	Missile Hardpoints: 8	Shield Recharge: 10
Gun Energy: 160.00	Gun Recharge: 6.00	Primary Weapons: 2 Tachyon Cannons, Rear Pulse Turret

Wolverine

Released after 200 kills or upon reaching Mission 17, the Wolverine performs well in capital ship assaults. Its nearly perfect shield rating and armor class means that the vessel can handle plenty of punishment. Furthermore, with five primary weapons, the Wolverine can work through subsystems extremely fast. The Reverse Thrust ability helps provide a quick escape when such assaults don't go well.

Heavy dogfighting missions should be left to the more able fighters, specifically the Reaper (if available) or Patriot. The Wolverine, while durable, just can't match the maneuverability of the faster Coalition craft. Eight missile hardpoints, however, mean you can equip lots of locking missiles to eliminate fighters without having to necessarily keep them in your crosshairs for too long.

Type: Heavy Fighter	Clearance: Lieutenant Commander	Displacement: 3.9 tons
Speed Rating: 5	ECM: 20 secs.	Armor Class: 7
Shield Rating: 6	Afterburner Fuel: 120 secs.	Max Speed: 280.00
Agility Rating: 4	Decoys: 20	Special Features: Reverse Thrust
Acceleration Rating: 10	Missile Hardpoints: 8	Shield Recharge: 10
Gun Energy: 140.00	Gun Recharge: 9.00	Primary Weapons: 2 Collapser Cannons, 2 Laser Cannons, 1 Tachyon Cannon, Rear Pulse Turret

Coalition Fighters

The Coalition fighters contain nearly the same diversity as the Alliance fighter fleet. Fighters like the Azan, Lagg, and Saracen provide a difficult maneuverability challenge, while heavier craft such as the Haidar and the cloaking Basilisk require hefty weapons and special tactics.

Azan

A light fighter with high speed, acceleration, and agility ratings, the Coalition's Azan provides a tough dogfight challenge for all but the most maneuverable Alliance vessel. If you're up against the Azan, consider diverting additional power to the engines to keep up with the speedy craft.

Type: Light Fighter	Displacement: 2 tons	Armor Class: 5
Speed Rating: 8	Agility Rating: 9	Acceleration Rating: 8
Shield Rating: 7	Shield Recharge: 12.00	Primary Weapons: 2 Pulse Cannons, 2 Messon Blasters
Afterburner: 100.00	Gun Energy: 100.00	Gun Recharge: 10.00

Basilisk

The Coalition Black Guard's Basilisk fighter offers a unique challenge, no matter which Alliance craft you select. Superb in all ratings, the Basilisk also features the ability to cloak. When trailing one, make an effort to keep the Coalition fighter within your crosshairs at all times. Equip some Vagabond missiles if you expect to encounter the Basilisk, as it can retain a lock even after the ship has cloaked.

Type: Prototype Medium Fighter	Displacement: 4 tons	Armor Class: 7
Speed Rating: 9	Agility Rating: 9	Acceleration Rating: 9
Shield Rating: 9	Shield Recharge: 14.00	Primary Weapons: 2 Gatling Lasers, 2 Messon Blasters, 2 Rear Laser Cannons
Afterburner: 60.00	Gun Energy: 200.00	Gun Recharge: 10.00

Haidar

While durable and powerful, the Haidar heavy fighter shouldn't present a problem for the more maneuverable Alliance ships. Knock down its shields and finish off its durable hull with a constant stream of primary weapons. Because the Haidar is fairly sluggish, be sure to match speed so you don't overrun the target.

Type: Heavy Fighter	Displacement: 3 tons	Armor Class: 9
Speed Rating: 7	Agility Rating: 6	Acceleration Rating: 6
Shield Rating: 7	Shield Recharge: 12.00	Primary Weapons: 2 Gatling Lasers, 2 Laser Cannons, Rear Laser Cannon
Afterburner: 100.00	Gun Energy: 100.00	Gun Recharge: 10.00

Karak

Boasting excellent speed, shields, and primary weapons, the Karak can pose problems in numbers. In one-on-one situations, however, its low armor rating shouldn't be able to withstand the Alliance's more punishing dogfighting craft.

Type: Medium Fighter	Displacement: 3.2 tons	Armor Class: 6
Speed Rating: 9	Agility Rating: 7	Acceleration Rating: 7
Shield Rating: 9	Shield Recharge: 14.00	Primary Weapons: 2 Messon Blasters, 2 Proton Cannons, Rear Laser Cannon
Afterburner: 100.00	Gun Energy: 100.00	Gun Recharge: 10.00

Kossac

Similar to the Haidar, the Kossac heavy fighter boasts moderate speed and maneuverability. Agile Alliance fighters should have little trouble against the Kossac, particularly since its armor rating isn't quite as impressive as that boasted by the Haidar.

Type: Heavy Fighter	Displacement: 4 tons	Armor Class: 6
Speed Rating: 7	Agility Rating: 6	Acceleration Rating: 6
Shield Rating: 8	Shield Recharge: 15.00	Primary Weapons: 2 Vulcan Cannons, 2 Gatling Lasers, Rear Facing Twin Lasers
Afterburner: 60.00	Gun Energy: 100.00	Gun Recharge: 10.00

Lagg

One of the more prominent fighters in the Coalition fleet, the Lagg medium fighter will be encountered often. Matching its speed and acceleration rating requires an equally nimble Alliance ship. Be prepared for a tough battle if you're in a slower fighter such as the Grendel, Crusader, or Wolverine.

Type: Medium Fighter	Displacement: 2 tons	Armor Class: 6
Speed Rating: 8	Agility Rating: 7	Acceleration Rating: 8
Shield Rating: 9	Shield Recharge: 15.00	Primary Weapons: 2 Gatling Lasers, 2 Pulse Cannons
Afterburner: 100.00	Gun Energy: 100.00	Gun Recharge: 10.00

Sabre

Like the Coalition's Lagg fighter, the Sabre will be prominent in many missions. It features enough speed and maneuverability to pose problems for the heavier and slower Alliance ships. The Sabre's sleek design also presents a difficult target. Additionally, two rear laser cannons can wreak havoc on your forward shielding, so be prepared to adjust shields to protect your armor.

Type: Medium Fighter	Displacement: 3 tons	Armor Class: 8
Speed Rating: 6	Agility Rating: 7	Acceleration Rating: 6
Shield Rating: 8	Shield Recharge: 16.00	Primary Weapons: 2 Pulse Cannons, 2 Messon Blasters, 2 Rear Facing Laser Cannons
Afterburner: 100.00	Gun Energy: 100.00	Gun Recharge: 10.00

Saracen

Excluding the special Basilisk used by the Black Guard, the Saracen medium fighter is the most well-rounded ship in the Coalition fleet. Though it doesn't excel in any single area, its above average, balanced statistics create a difficult target for any Alliance pilot. Use secondary weapons to knife into the Saracen's shields, then follow up with primary weapons upon entering close range. Most Alliance fighters should be able to keep up with the Saracen, as it isn't particularly fast.

Type: Medium Fighter	Displacement: 2 tons	Armor Class: 7
Speed Rating: 7	Agility Rating: 8	Acceleration Rating: 7
Shield Rating: 8	Shield Recharge: 14.00	Primary Weapons: 2 Pulse Cannons, 2 Proton Cannons, 2 Rear Facing Pulse Cannons
Afterburner: 100.00	Gun Energy: 100.00	Gun Recharge: 10.00

chapter 4

Weapon Strategies and Statistics

Having mastered the skills of flight, survived dangerous dogfighting challenges, and improved your piloting skills, you're now prepared to start using live rounds within the context of weapons training. Informed decisions about weapon selection can turn difficult combat situations into cakewalks. Conversely, you're apt to face an uphill battle if you make the wrong decision.

In this chapter, you'll find the complete list of primary and secondary weapons available in *StarLancer*. Each gun and missile entry includes detailed statistics on projectile speed, damage potential, rate of fire, power use, range, and lock times, as well as in-depth combat strategies and suggestions for use. Skilled use of primary and secondary weapons greatly affects mission outcome. Study the techniques offered here to improve your single- and multiplayer experiences.

Weapon Statistics Explained

The weaponry discussed below have been separated into primary weapons (guns) and secondary weapons (missiles). The table accompanying each weapon description and strategy displays a series of important statistics. Below is an explanation of the terms used in the tables:

 Range: The distance before the projectile dissipates. In terms of secondary weapons, it's the number of seconds before the missile expires and blows up after launching.

 Speed: The velocity of the projectile. Multiply the table number by four for game distance units per second.

 Shield Damage: Relative damage inflicted to shield strength.

 Armor Damage: Relative damage that the shot inflicts to hull armor.

 Rate of Fire: Relative firing frequency of the weapon. The higher the number, the faster the weapon can fire.

Power Use: Relative amount of gun energy consumed by the weapon.

Missiles per Hardpoint: The number of missiles that can be attached to a single ship hardpoint.

Lock Time: Time it takes to acquire a missile lock represented in 1/100th of a second.

 Pitch Rate: The rate at which a missile can turn. The higher the number, the faster the missile turns and the more maneuverable it is.

 Chaff Percentage: The probability a missile will be fooled by a decoy. The higher the percentage, the more likely.

Lock Distance: Game distance units at which the missile lock is effective.

Guns

StarLancer's primary weapons include energy (which use the fighter's gun energy reserves) and ballistic armaments (which use limited ammunition, such as missiles). All ships include at least one primary weapon type, while others include several. Unlike most missiles, primary weapons (or guns) don't require target locks and will never run out of ammunition as long as you keep power flowing to your ship's gun energy reserve.

In this section, you'll find descriptions and complete statistics for *StarLancer*'s primary

warning

Powering your fighter's gun system should usually be among the least of your concerns. Unless you're using a ship equipped with weapons that draw a great deal of power, such as the Neutron Particle Gun or the Tachyon Cannon, you'll never really have to worry about gun reserve depletion. Use the power distribution system to divert some power from the guns to the shields, often a more important asset in combat situations.

weapons. Use the ship tables in Chapter 3, "Ship Strategies and Statistics," to discover what each vessel is equipped with. Compare the results with the damage potentials of each weapon—listed in the tables in this section—to discover each ship's relative primary weapon firepower.

Collapser Guns

A powerful ballistic weapon with a medium range, the Collapser Gun utilizes explosive-tipped projectiles to penetrate hull armor to maximum effect. Heavy damage to shield and armor coupled with no power use makes for a most effective weapon.

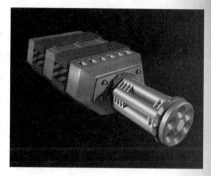

Range: 200.00

Armor Damage: 25.00

Speed: 1400.00

Rate of Fire: 6.00

Shield Damage: 25.00

Power Use: 0.00

Gatling Lasers

A heavyweight short range weapon with an awesome fire rate. The Gatling achieves this with multiple laser generators that charge and fire almost instantly. Though it doesn't quite pack the damage potential of other guns, its superb rate of fire more than compensates for this shortcoming.

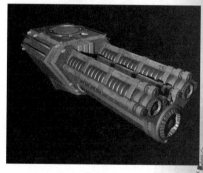

Range: 140.00

Armor Damage: 6.00

Speed: 1800.00

Rate of Fire: 10.00

Shield Damage: 8.50

Power Use: 2.00

Gatling Plasma Cannon

A hard-hitting projectile weapon with an adequate fire rate. Its power-driven breach can fire a continuous stream of depleted plasma rounds from its multi-barreled chamber. Decent range, adequate damage rating, and no power use round out this effective cannon.

Range: 200.00

Armor Damage: 7.00

Speed: 1200.00

Rate of Fire: 5.00

Shield Damage: 10.00

Power Use: 0.00

Laser Cannon

The standard light armament for all Alliance fighter craft. An efficient and reliable short range weapon with low energy consumption and a high fire rate.

Range: 200.00

Armor Damage: 8.00

Speed: 1600.00

Rate of Fire: 5.50

Shield Damage: 8.00

Power Use: 2.00

Messon Blaster

A medium range weapon that incorporates a super cooled lens condenser to focus the energy beam more accurately and with more power over a longer range.

Range: 150.00

Armor Damage: 9.00

Speed: 1300.00

Rate of Fire: 8.00

Shield Damage: 9.00

Power Use: 2.00

Neutron Particle Gun

The Neutron Particle Gun has a high yield energy delivery system, but a relatively slow fire rate. However, the damage potential makes it a very powerful energy weapon at close or medium range. Be prepared to divert additional power to the gun systems to compensate for the gun's usage.

Range: 200.00

Armor Damage: 30.00

Speed: 1300.00

Rate of Fire: 2.00

Shield Damage: 35.00

Power Use: 15.00

Nova Cannon

The power output of this weapon depends on how long the trigger is held before firing. A heavy charge causes massive damage, but greedily consumes power. The Nova Cannon is a special weapon only available on the Alliance Phoenix fighter.

Range: 200.00

Armor Damage: 400.00

Speed: 2000.00

Rate of Fire: 0.01

Shield Damage: 400.00

Power Use: Special

Proton Cannon

A short-range energy weapon with a good damage rate per hit. The Proton Cannon has a low loss energy firing chamber, which creates an efficient charge but lowers its rate of fire.

Range: 200.00	
Armor Damage: 11.00	
Speed: 1500.00	
Rate of Fire: 6.00	
Shield Damage: 12.00	
Power Use: 3.00	

Pulse Cannon

This energy weapon makes use of a pulse accelerator unit to deliver a more powerful charge than the standard laser cannon.

Range: 300.00	
Armor Damage: 8.00	
Speed: 1400.00	
Rate of Fire: 8.00	
Shield Damage: 8.00	
Power Use: 3.00	

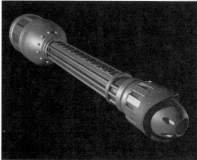

Tachyon Cannon

This weapon energizes Tachyon particles, which disrupt matter fields and cause substances to destabilize at the atomic level. Drawbacks are its heavy power drain and slow recharge rate. Expect to divert additional power to the gun systems to compensate, particularly with two such cannons on board.

Range: 400.00	
Armor Damage: 15.00	
Speed: 1400.00	
Rate of Fire: 5.00	
Shield Damage: 20.00	
Power Use: 5.00	

Vulcan Battery

This gun has a high fire rate and the greatest destructive capability of all the ballistic weapons. Uranium tipped shells ensure maximum damage to enemy shield strength and hull armor.

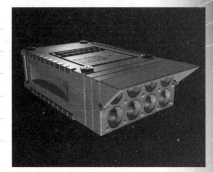

Range: 300.00	
Armor Damage: 35.00	
Speed: 1700.00	
Rate of Fire: 2.00	
Shield Damage: 30.00	
Power Use: 0.00	

Missiles

StarLancer's secondary weapons include warheads and pods which can be attached to any fighter's open hardpoints. These categories include various types of missiles and fuel pods. As each fighter can only hold a certain number of missiles or pods, you must choose wisely so you have enough of the correct armaments to complete the mission's task.

Much like *StarLancer*'s playable fighters, only some secondary weapons are offered at the beginning of the campaign. As you successfully complete certain milestones, you're offered more powerful warheads. Table 4.1 illustrates which missiles become available by completing the designated mission.

note

Some missiles don't require target locks. For instance, the Screamer dumb fire and the Solomon fire-and-forget can be used without a target lock. *StarLancer*'s other missiles, however, can only be fired once you've obtained a lock.

Table 4.1 : Missile Release Schedule

Level	Release Point	New Missiles Available
Bronze	Game Start	Bandit, Fuel Pod, Havoc, Jackhammer, Screamer
Silver	Start Mission 12	Imp, Raptor, Vagabond
Gold	Start Mission 17	Hawk
Platinum	Start Mission 19	Solomon

This section includes descriptions, strategies, and complete statistics for all secondary weapons found in the game. Use the ship tables in Chapter 3, "Ship Strategies and Statistics," to discover how many missile hardpoints each fighter contains. Armed with this information, you can make informed decisions about which missiles to equip and which missiles to ignore.

Bandit

Available at the beginning of the *StarLancer* campaign, the Bandit serves as your principal dogfighting missile during the early missions. Though you receive only one missile per hardpoint, equip at least a couple of Bandits for each of the game's early missions. Once you acquire the Raptor—released by reaching Mission 12—you should no longer need the Bandit's services.

Featuring excellent velocity and delivering solid damage to both shields and armor, the Bandit's primary weakness is its relatively long lock time. To achieve a Bandit lock, you must keep your crosshairs on the enemy ship for a full second over the next potent dogfighting missile.

Range: 60.00	
Lock Time: 500.00	
Speed: 500.00	
Pitch Rate: 0.14	
Shield Damage: 220.00	
Chaff Percentage: 20.00	
Armor Damage: 200.00	
Lock Distance: 100.00	
Missiles per Hardpoint: 1	

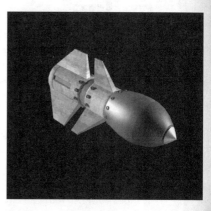

Fuel Pod

Similar to the fuel drop tanks used by World War II aircraft, *StarLancer*'s Fuel Pod, offered from the start of the campaign, can be outfitted to any available hardpoint to add an additional 50 units of afterburner fuel. Sacrificing a hardpoint, and thus a missile, for fuel is risky, particularly in the early part of the campaign where effective dogfighting missiles are rarer. But, if you wish to select a more powerful, durable fighter that lacks speed and afterburner fuel, the Fuel Pod helps compensate for those weaknesses.

Consider Fuel Pods in torpedo interception and escort missions where you can expect to utilize the afterburner fre-

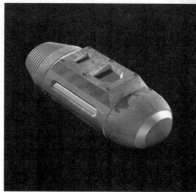

quently. Running out of afterburner fuel mid-mission often spells disaster against the dangers that always arrive near the end.

Havoc

The Havoc warhead, available from the beginning of *StarLancer*'s campaign, offers more than your standard damage potential. It explodes a short distance from enemy targets, emitting a shockwave that temporarily knocks out the victims' electrical systems. Any ship within the shockwave loses movement, speed, and weapons control. Any vessel affected is basically a sitting duck until it recovers!

Select the Havoc on escort missions where you expect the Coalition to send waves of fighters and bombers at friendly cargo and capital ships. It works best when fired at a cluster of enemy fighters, especially as they enter the mission area. Shutting their systems down like this gives you additional time to use primary weapons and missiles to eliminate the enemy fighters once and for all.

Range: 80.00	
Lock Time: 300.00	
Speed: 400.00	
Pitch Rate: 0.16	
Shield Damage: 300.00	
Chaff Percentage: 20.00	
Armor Damage: 200.00	
Lock Distance: 100.00	
Missiles per Hardpoint: 1	

Hawk

Released upon reaching Mission 17, the Hawk serves as the primary dogfighting warhead through the latter stages of the campaign against the Coalition. With four missiles for each hardpoint, you can get a lot of mileage out of the Hawk, especially when flying an Alliance fighter containing ample hardpoints.

Though its damage potential to shields and armor can't match the Raptor or even the Bandit, the Hawk does feature excellent range and lock distance. This allows you to achieve a lock from a greater distance and still expect the warhead to reach its target. However, since the Hawk inflicts less damage per missile, plan on using more than one per enemy fighter.

Range: 120.00

Lock Time: 400.00

Speed: 400.00

Pitch Rate: 0.14

Shield Damage: 120.00

Chaff Percentage: 30.00

Armor Damage: 120.00

Lock Distance: 300.00

Missiles per Hardpoint: 4

Imp

Available at the beginning of Mission 12, the Imp missile operates similarly to its Havoc cousin. The Imp explodes a short distance from enemy targets and destroys or disables the shields of any enemy ships within its blast zone. Because the Imp requires a full missile hardpoint for use, you shouldn't equip too many. Select them particularly for escort missions where you can assume you'll become overwhelmed by enemy fighters and bombers.

Follow up the Imp missile with additional dogfighting warheads such as the Raptor. Combine the Imp with savvy fighter selection, looking particularly for fighters with powerful primary weapons against hull armor (such as Vulcan Batteries, Tachyon Cannons, or Neutron Particle Guns).

Range: 60.00

Lock Time: 200.00

Speed: 500.00

Pitch Rate: 0.18

Shield Damage: 240.00

Chaff Percentage: 40.00

Armor Damage: 240.00

Lock Distance: 100.00

Missiles per Hardpoint: 1

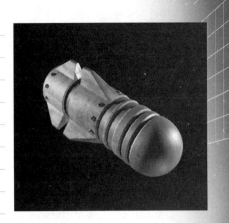

Jackhammer

The largest warhead presented for the Alliance fighters, the Jackhammer offers the largest damage potential out of all missiles available in the game. However, high lock time, low speed, high chaff percentage, and very little maneuverability offset its power. Therefore, hold the Jackhammer for larger, more static targets such as pickup ships, Kurgen corvettes, and other cargo vessels.

Don't even attempt to use this slow warhead against Coalition fighters—even the sluggish vessels like the Haidar. Unless the fighter is already damaged, it won't have much problem out-maneuvering the Jackhammer. In a pinch, you could use the Jackhammer against slow torpedo bombers, though even that's overkill.

Range: 80.00

Lock Time: 600.00

Speed: 240.00

Pitch Rate: 0.10

Shield Damage: 2501.00

Chaff Percentage: 40.00

Armor Damage: 2501.00

Lock Distance: 100.00

Missiles per Hardpoint: 1

Raptor

Offered after reaching Mission 12, the Raptor serves as your principal dogfighting missile during the middle missions. It also remains useful through the entire course of the campaign. Though it only offers three missiles per hardpoint compared to the Hawk, which offers four, the Raptor's higher speed and damage potential succeeds better in destroying enemy fighters quickly.

The Raptor's short range and lock distance (nearly the opposite of the Hawk) requires you to closely approach the enemy. Line up your shots with this warhead carefully so that the explosive payload reaches its target.

Range: 50.00

Lock Time: 300.00

Speed: 500.00

Pitch Rate: 0.20

Shield Damage: 250.00

Chaff Percentage: 30.00

Armor Damage: 200.00

Lock Distance: 160.00

Missiles per Hardpoint: 3

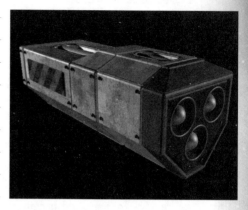

Screamer

Available from the start of the *StarLancer* campaign, Screamers are known as "dumb fire" missiles, because they don't require a target lock and don't adjust trajectory once launched. It operates much like a primary weapon—simply point and shoot. Though the Screamer doesn't inflict much damage per warhead in comparison to other missiles, you receive 20 Screamers per hardpoint. Couple its quantity with its high rate-of-fire and the Screamer carries decent damage potential.

You'll likely hold Screamer missiles for static targets, such as Kurgens, bombers, capital ship subtargets, or pickup ships. However, Screamers are also moderately effective against mobile enemy fighters. Fire them as you would your ship's guns. Approach within close-range and launch them at the primary weapon lead indicator.

Range: 60.00

Speed: 500.00

Shield Damage: 80.00

Chaff Percentage: 40.00

Armor Damage: 80.00

Missiles per Hardpoint: 20

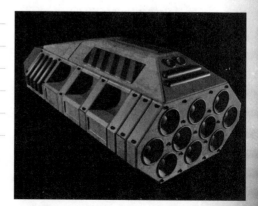

Solomon

The Solomon missile, offered upon reaching Mission 19, is one of two *StarLancer* missiles that doesn't require a target lock. Unlike the Screamer, however, the Solomon locks onto the nearest enemy target, upon launch. The nearest enemy could include fighters, bombers, and even torpedoes. With four missiles per hardpoint, the Solomon is one of the best dogfighting missiles to use in the latter missions.

Although the Solomon offers many advantages, including solid damage and speed, these advantages are somewhat offset by a relatively low range and an extremely high decoy percentage. While it has no trouble locking onto the nearest enemy fighter, the missile is easily fooled by countermeasures. Cut down this possibility by launching the Solomon close to enemy targets.

Range: 60.00

Speed: 400.00

Pitch Rate: 0.14

Shield Damage: 200.00

Chaff Percentage: 80.00

Armor Damage: 100.00

Missiles per Hardpoint: 4

Vagabond

Available upon reaching Mission 12, the Vagabond offers the highest damage potential of any dogfighting missile. The down side of this is that your fighter can hold only one Vagabond per hardpoint. Also, the warhead's low pitch rate means that it's less maneuverable than other dogfighting missiles and it's less likely to strike its target.

The Vagabond's most important feature is its ability to remain locked onto a stealth ship even after it has cloaked. This means that upon receiving a target lock on a non-cloaked ship and launching the Vagabond, the missile will remain locked on and could still impact on the target even if the target cloaks. Therefore, consider the Vagabond when you expect cloaked enemies, such as the Black Guard Basilisk fighters.

Range: 100.00

Lock Time: 400.00

Speed: 600.00

Pitch Rate: 0.12

Shield Damage: 500.00

Chaff Percentage: 20.00

Armor Damage: 350.00

Lock Distance: 140.00

Missiles per Hardpoint: 1

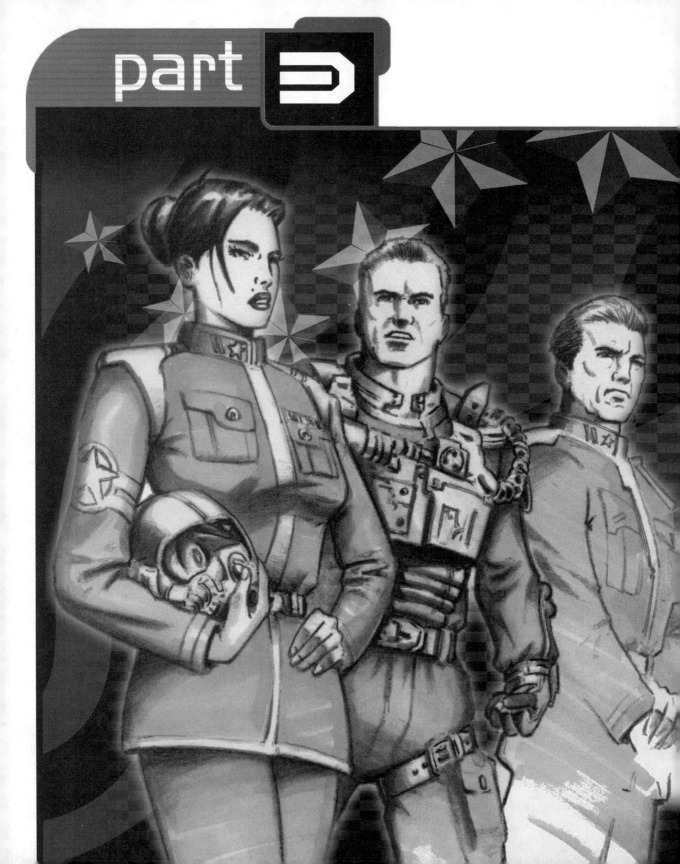

part 3

Alliance Missions:

Tour of Duty

With combat, ship, and weapon training under your flight belt, it's time to become part of the 45th Volunteers and fight alongside brave Alliance pilots as they battle the nefarious Coalition. "Part 3— Alliance Missions: Tour of Duty" covers all of *StarLancer*'s single-player sorties. Each mission walkthrough contains the complete briefing, recommended ship selection and missile load out, tactics for completing each objective, and a rundown of mission success and failure conditions.

Chapter 5 covers *StarLancer*'s first campaign, comprising the game's first seven missions. Chapter 6 offers walkthroughs and strategies for the four missions that make up the second campaign. Head into Chapter 7 for tactics covering the five missions of the third campaign. Chapter 8 includes walkthroughs for the two mission-long fourth campaign, while Chapter 9 offers strategies for the three missions that await you in the fifth campaign. Proceed to Chapter 10 for walkthroughs of the three missions that comprise the sixth and final campaign in *StarLancer*.

chapter 5

Retreat to Triton— Missions 1 to 7

The Alliance continues to struggle in its war with the Coalition. Supplies, including missiles, ships, and even pilots, are running low. You're part of the 45th Volunteers, a ragtag group of inexperienced squadron pilots thrown together to assist in a wide variety of sorties.

You'll find walkthroughs for *StarLancer*'s first seven missions inside this chapter. The missions comprise the game's first campaign, an introduction of sorts where you're given the chance to prove yourself in battle with a set of basic ships and secondary weapons. Learn the elements of dogfighting and torpedo interception before tackling this campaign. Not only will you face dozens of agile Coalition fighters, but you must defend several convoys and civilian ships from vicious torpedo attacks.

Mission 1

Mission Date: June 24, 2160

Briefing: This is Operation Shield, the aim of which is to secure the surrounding area and protect any Alliance ships going to Neptune's moon Triton. The 45th Volunteer Squadron is assigned a British convoy consisting of one heavy cargo carrier and a number of light transports.

Rendezvous with the convoy. Once you've made contact, take up escort position and provide fighter cover until you reach Fort Sherman. Make sure they arrive at Neptune in one piece. If you encounter the enemy, torpedo bombers are your first priority; fighters are secondary.

Ship Selection and Missile Load Out

This is your first mission apart from simulated training exercises, but you shouldn't have too much trouble successfully completing Mission 1 with any of the available fighters. The Alliance isn't going to dump you on the front lines quite yet.

In this mission you'll battle two waves of quick Coalition Sabres and eliminate a series of slow, small torpedoes launched from an even slower bomber. A Black Guard pilot in the cockpit of a cloaking Coalition Basilisk is also offered up as a difficult bonus target.

Although any load out should be effective, your best bet is to take speed and Blind Fire capabilities over firepower. Select the Predator, an agile, but weakly armored ship. Its speed advantage over the Sabres and its Blind Fire special ability provides an edge over all Coalition targets, especially the Black Guard fighter, found in this mission.

Unload the Screamer pods from the Predator's hardpoints. Though you get 20 missiles with each pod, the non-locking Screamers aren't effective against the quick Coalition Sabres; you're wiser to free up hardpoints for additional locking missiles in case any torpedoes sneak by. Replace the Screamer pods with Bandit missiles for use against the Sabres. If you desire to eliminate the torpedo bomber quickly, take one Screamer for use against its armored hull.

Battle Plan

Objective: Rendezvous with the convoy.

Your first priority upon launching from the *ANS Reliant* is to locate the convoy. Before engaging your jump drive engines, take time to meet your fellow pilots in the 45th and become familiar with *StarLancer*'s heads-up display.

Along with the basic elements of flight, speed, and attack, this first mission requires cycling through missile types, sending orders to Alpha wingmen, and an adept use of the targeting system. Press the missile-display button to open the missile window and then use the rotation keys to cycle through available missiles. Open up the communication display to issue orders to specific Alpha wingmen or to all of the wingmen at once. Finally, use the target-nearest-enemy and target-torpedo buttons when locking on enemy fighters, bombers, and torpedoes.

When you're ready for battle—and once your copilot Moose gives the go ahead—engage your jump drive to proceed to the next mission area. Upon emerging, you'll spot the Alliance convoy, consisting of one Nanny, one Mammoth, and two Leuneberg cargo vessels. Receive the order to enter escort formation and locate the red wire frame cylinder (denoting the escort position) above the Nanny ship. Fly inside to automatically switch to escort velocity (see Figure 5.1).

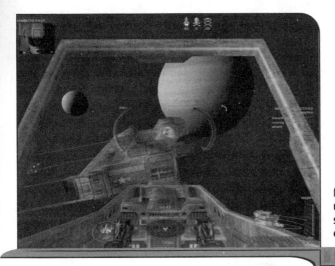

Figure 5.1: Fly into the red wire frame to automatically synchronize your speed to the convoy's lead ship.

Once you've approached the convoy and entered escort position, listen to the radio chatter as your wingmen and the Mammoth pilot discuss Coalition activities in the area. Only a moment after the conversation begins, a member of the Coalition's infamous Black Guard, piloting a cloaked Basilisk fighter, ambushes one of your wingmen. Dealing with this Black Guard pilot isn't a mission requirement, but destroying his Basilisk will complete a bonus objective.

Before the ambush cut-scene, you may wish to open the missile display and select your Bandit missiles. Eliminating the pesky Black Guard fighter requires launching a volley of missiles into its hull.

Bonus Objective: Eliminate the Black

Guard pilot.
After the cut-scene of the Black Guard fighter's entrance, immediately press the target-nearest-fighter button to highlight his Basilisk in your targeting display. Use the target direction indicator (the red arrow around your crosshairs) to locate its position relative to your own. As soon as you're heading toward the Basilisk, press the afterburner button and match speed. You need to approach its position as quickly as possible.

As you approach the Black Guard pilot, he'll cloak his Basilisk fighter and disappear from both your sight and targeting display. Back off on the afterburner, but keep moving full speed toward his last position.

The Basilisk pilot will then use his communication system to taunt you and your fellow wingmen. Target the vessel as it uncloaks, achieve a missile lock (if you haven't already), and begin firing. Match its speed and pound the craft with your primary weapons. The Predator's Blind Fire ability makes destroying the Black Guard ship easier, as long as you close quickly to less than 80 meters. Don't hesitate here. If you wait too long before attacking, the Basilisk will flee the mission area and you'll lose the chance to complete this bonus objective.

Objective: Escort and protect the convoy from enemy attack.

After the Black Guard fighter is either destroyed or jumps from the mission area, six Coalition Sabres enter to assault the convoy. Immediately target the nearest Sabre and intercept it using your ship's afterburner or by diverting power to the engines. Be sure to match your target's speed as you approach—matching speed prevents you from overshooting your target and you should have an easier time keeping the enemy ship in your crosshairs.

Once the initial six Sabres are destroyed, an additional four enter escorting a lone torpedo bomber. Order your wingmen to attack specific Sabre fighters, as this will draw the enemy ships off your tail while you engage the torpedo bomber. Cycle through the enemy targets to locate the bomber, or use the target-nearest-torpedo key, and use your afterburner to intercept the ship.

By the time you reach the torpedo bomber, it will have likely fired one or two torpedoes on the convoy vessels. Ignore the bomber when torpedoes have been launched; protect the convoy by eliminating the torpedoes first, then worry about destroying the bomber (see Figure 5.2).

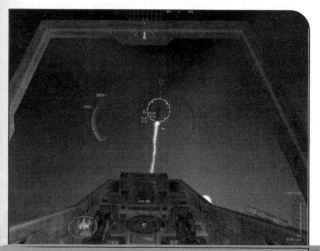

Figure 5.2: The torpedoes are your biggest priority. Destroy them, then go after the torpedo bomber itself.

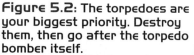

You can either cycle through enemy targets or press the target-torpedo-shortcut key to target the bombs. A torpedo's small size presents a difficult target. Attack them from the rear by pursuing its bright trail, firing your weapons into the center of the trail to strike the torpedo. Alternatively, you can come over the top of the torpedoes as you approach. Just be careful that you don't accidentally ram one. Save some locking missiles for use in destroying the torpedoes before they can reach the convoy.

Completing Mission 1 successfully requires saving at least two of the four convoy vessels. If you have trouble intercepting the torpedoes, use the communication display to order wingmen to engage the torpedo bomber and the torpedoes. Once the bomber and its fighter escort are destroyed, the convoy jumps to the next mission area and orders you to Fort Sherman.

> **tip**
>
> After targeting a torpedo, press the match-speed key. Approach the torpedo by hitting the afterburner key, then return to normal speed as you get close. If you don't match speed, you might overrun the torpedo or, even worse, smash into it, instantly destroying your fighter.

Mission Debriefing

 Success plus Bonus: All cargo ships survive and Black Guard fighter destroyed.

 Success: All cargo ships survive.

Partial Success: Two cargo ships survive.

Partial Fail: One cargo ship survives.

Fail: All cargo ships destroyed.

Mission 2

Mission Date: July 10, 2160

Briefing: Neptune is the primary destination for the remnants of the Alliance fleet and, consequently, a hot zone for Coalition hunter-killer squadrons. Your mission is to sweep the surrounding quadrants for any incoming Alliance vessels and escort them to Fort Baxter.

You will not be alone on this mission. Operations Command thinks it's a good idea if you link up with a veteran outfit, an American squadron called the Pumas. They want you to learn from professionals. The Puma squadron leader, Jake Tanner, will be in full command of this mission.

Ship Selection and Missile Load Out

An attack against a well-armored pickup ship and intense dogfighting against nearly two dozen swift fighters dominates your second mission. Much like the first mission, you should be able to perform well by selecting any ship and configuration. The Predator's Blind Fire ability certainly proves effective against the fighters, although selecting a more heavily-armed fighter—both with a better primary weapon and a greater quantity of hardpoints—works equally well.

Opt for the Crusader over the Predator because of its increased primary firepower (two gatling lasers) and its increased missile capacity. Although the Crusader isn't quite as mobile as the Predator, the greater number of armaments, better shielding, and extra afterburner fuel will make up for its lack of agility and Blind Fire. Also, the Crusader's Spectral Shields special ability provides extra defense when dogfighting around two Coalition cruisers later in the mission.

Keep one of the Screamer missile pods for use against the Antonov pickup ship. Load the Crusader's other missile hardpoints with Bandit missiles; out of the available secondary weapons, the Bandits are the most effective against the agile Coalition fighters you'll face in this mission.

Battle Plan

Objective: Rendezvous with the Pumas at the *ANS Washington.* Patrol the surrounding area. Launch from the *Reliant* and, once your wingmen give the order, activate your jump drive. Upon entering the next mission area, you'll meet Colonel Jake Tanner and the other Pumas. Approach the *ANS Washington* and prepare for orders. After you're introduced to the Pumas, General Briggs radios for help—his Prowler is under attack by Coalition forces. The Pumas order your wing to intercept and engage. Press the jump-drive key when prompted.

You'll find General Briggs' Prowler nearly destroyed as you enter the next area. Several Coalition Sabre fighters disengage from the battle and exit the mission area as soon as your superior force arrives. If you target the nearest Sabre and use the afterburner, you can destroy it—though it's not required—before it jumps. Tanner notifies the wings that General Briggs' escape pod has jettisoned from the Prowler. He orders an Alliance Nanny pickup ship to retrieve the pod.

Objective: Destroy the Antonov pickup ship.
Unfortunately, a Coalition Antonov pickup ship, escorted by eight Saracen fighters, responds to the call. Eliminating the Antonov before it acquires the escape pod completes part of the mission's bonus objective. Ignore the escort fighters and target the Antonov as soon as it enters the mission area. Turn your crosshairs toward the pickup ship and slow down so you don't ram the slow-moving vessel. As you approach, tear apart its hull with both primary weapons and Screamer missiles (see Figure 5.3).

Figure 5.3: Target the Antonov as soon as it enters the mission area and pummel it with Screamer missiles.

You must act quickly, as it won't take the Antonov long to grab the General's escape pod. If you fail to prevent the Coalition ship from grabbing the pod, you won't be able to complete the mission's bonus objective of protecting the convoy and saving General Briggs from capture or death.

Objective: Destroy the Antonov's fighter escort.

Once the Antonov is eliminated, turn your attention to the remaining Saracen fighters. You'll face a tougher battle near the end of the mission, so conserve as much afterburner fuel and as many missiles as you can by eliminating the Saracens with primary weapons alone. With the fighters destroyed, the Pumas request a long-range scan of the area. Allied Command reports a Coalition hunting pack en route to an Alliance convoy. Follow the Pumas to the next area with your jump drive.

Objective: Protect the convoy from attack.

One Kestral and two Mammoth cargo vessels await your arrival. Enter escort position by flying inside the red wire frame behind the Kestral. Hornet wing, under attack further ahead, radios for backup and the Pumas jump to assist, leaving you to escort the convoy. After a few blurbs of radio chatter, a wing of seven Coalition fighters enters to assault the convoy.

Target the nearest fighter and engage. Watch the communication display as one of your wingmen announces the arrival of a Coalition torpedo bomber, which immediately targets the two Mammoth cargo ships. Ignore the fighters (assign your wingmen specific fighter targets if you wish) and use the target torpedo shortcut to locate the bomber. Use the afterburner to approach the bomber quickly and intercept any launched torpedoes. You must protect the convoy from the torpedoes to complete the mission with success. With the bomber destroyed, engage the remaining fighters. Once all Coalition vessels are eliminated, Col. Tanner radios from the next mission area and calls for assistance.

> **tip**
>
> Completing the bonus objective in Mission 2 requires saving General Briggs' escape pod and protecting both of the Mammoth cargo ships. If both Mammoths are destroyed, you automatically fail the mission.

Objective: Destroy the *Kirov's* fighter contingent.

Jump into the next area and find Col. Tanner and the Pumas engaged with six Coalition Azan fighters and a Coalition cruiser, the *Kirov*. Target the nearest Azan and engage. Order your wingmen against individual Azan targets to keep Coalition fighters off your back. Keep your distance from the cruiser and don't bother attempting to attack it (see Figure 5.4).

If you must get close to the cruiser in order to engage the Azan fighters, engage your Spectral Shields (if available) or ECM. Destroying the Azan fighters triggers the next events; so leave the cruiser alone as it will be destroyed shortly without any extra effort from you.

Objective: Destroy the *Zakov's* fighter contingent.

With the Azans eliminated, a second cruiser, the *Zakov*, enters the area and launches eight Lagg fighters. Once again, keep away from the cruisers and engage each fighter in turn. Eliminating the agile Coalition vessels requires an ample supply of afterburner fuel and locking missiles. Save as much of each during earlier battles to make these final engagements easier. When all Coalition fighters are

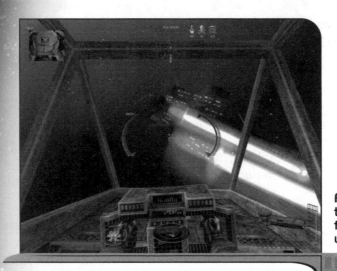

Figure 5.4: Stay away from the Coalition cruiser while dog-fighting the fighters. The cruiser will be destroyed soon enough.

destroyed, Captain Mukai pilots the *ANS Yamato* into the mission area and annihilates the two cruisers with torpedoes. Return to the *Reliant* and land to complete the mission successfully.

Mission Debriefing

 Success plus Bonus: Two Mammoths survive and General Briggs saved.

 Success: Both Mammoths saved.

Partial Success: One Mammoth saved.

Partial Success: One Mammoth saved and General Briggs saved.

Fail: Both Mammoths destroyed.

Mission 3

Mission Date: July 19, 2160

Briefing: The 45th must locate a flight recorder from a missing Alliance Command ship named the *Mantis*. The signal from the *Mantis* was lost moments after she began transmitting a distress call. Intelligence is concerned that a Coalition group may be working behind the lines. The 45th provides backup for top guns, the Vampires. Senior officer on the mission is squadron leader Klaus Steiner.

Your first objective will be to rendezvous with the Vampires and sweep the area around the last known position of the *Mantis*. Once the flight recorder has been located, return to base immediately. Intelligence has placed a high priority on the mission and wants the flight data recorder to ascertain what happened to the *Mantis*.

Ship Selection and Missile Load Out

This mission requires a ship with the agility and firepower to keep up with speedy Coalition Sabre fighters as well as the endurance to withstand punishment as you eliminate two relatively stationary targets. The Predator and Naginata are quick, but lack the weaponry and durability to match the Coalition forces you'll encounter in this mission.

Your choice lies with either the Crusader or the Grendel. Both should prove effective during the mission. Select the Crusader if you prefer a slight mobility advantage to minor shield and armor short-comings. The Grendel should be your choice if you favor durability over agility; furthermore, the Grendel carries two additional missile hardpoints for increased firepower.

Outfit your fighter with one Screamer pod for use against the mission's two main targets, the Prototype Warp Gate power source and the science vessel's engines. The powerful, but sluggish, Jackhammer missile will also prove effective against the two slow or non-moving targets. Load up the other missile hardpoints with Bandit missiles to use against the Coalition fighters.

Battle Plan

Objective: Fly to the *Bremen* and rendezvous with Steiner.

Exit the *Reliant* and jump to the next mission area to rendezvous with the *ANS Bremen*. Shortly after you arrive, Klaus Steiner will emerge from the carrier in his Wolverine fighter (to the jealousy of the 45th wingmen). Listen to Steiner's prediction of a smooth ride to the *Mantis* debris and follow his wing when he engages the jump drive.

warning

Don't dawdle in assisting the Leuneberg—the Coalition fighters will continue to pound the freighter until you intercept them. Order your wingmen to engage specific enemy craft to keep them all occupied.

Objective: Move out to find the *Mantis*.

The search for the *Mantis*'s flight recorder takes a brief detour when you're pulled out of the jump to respond to distress calls from a Leuneberg freighter under attack by eight Coalition Lagg fighters. Immediately target and engage the nearest Lagg. Completing the bonus objective in Mission 2 requires saving General Briggs' escape pod and protecting both of the Mammoth cargo ships. If both Mammoths are destroyed, you automatically fail the mission.

Once the area is secure, the freighter captain will thank you. Steiner will wonder aloud how Coalition fighters were able to enter this area when long-range scanners revealed no Coalition carriers. Follow Steiner when he engages his jump drive to enter the next mission point.

Objective: Locate and retrieve the Command ship's flight recorder.

You'll spot the *Mantis* debris field up ahead. Immediately slow your fighter and head toward the debris field. As you approach, Steiner will announce that the Coalition has booby-trapped the field with proximity mines. Don't charge into the minefield looking for the flight recorder. Slow down and wait until you automatically target the first mine (see Figure 5.5). Alternatively, you can use the target-nearest-enemy shortcut to target the mines as soon as you jump in. Destroy each mine as it shows up on your screen, then proceed with the search for the flight recorder.

To locate the flight recorder, slowly guide your ship through the debris field and listen for the scanner's beeping. The faster the beeping,

Figure 5.5: Approach the proximity mines slowly and eliminate them before searching for the flight recorder.

the closer you are to the flight recorder. You can spot the recorder easily against the blackness of space; it has a red and green light flashing around its center. Pilot your ship toward the device and watch the cut-scene of the Coalition science vessel warping in through the anomaly. Seconds later, you're pulled inside that same anomaly.

Objective: Destroy the Coalition's Warp Prototype Warp Gate core.

The anomaly pulls you through a Coalition Prototype Warp Gate, designed to allow Coalition ships to fly quickly through various systems without the need of a carrier. You'll emerge near Venus at what looks like a Coalition outpost. A wing of six Coalition fighters immediately attacks.

Though Klaus Steiner will order you to attack the Prototype Warp Gate's power core, take the time to eliminate a few of the Coalition fighters first. Order your wingmen to engage individual Coalition ships and destroy two or three fighters yourself. Attempting to take out the Prototype Warp Gate's power source with all six enemy fighters active poses problems because you simply can't attack the power source without taking significant damage to your rear shielding. Also, don't eliminate all of the Coalition fighters protecting the Warp Gate. Leave at least one, because if you destroy them all, another wing of Sabre fighters emerges to prevent the destruction of the gate.

Once you've thinned the enemy ranks, divert additional power to your fighter's shields for protection against the remaining fighters and face the Prototype Warp Gate. The rotating oval-shaped area on the gate's side is your target. You may need to keep a solid supply of power running to your ship's gun system, though, to keep your primary weapons recharged and firing upon the gate. Pummel the armor plating around the core with guns and Screamer missiles (see Figure 5.6). Once exposed, you can knock out the Prototype Warp Gate by firing at the center of the core.

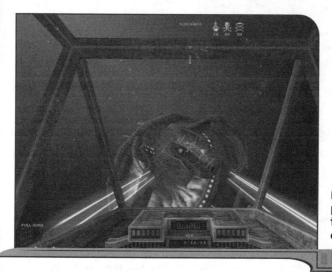

Figure 5.6: Target the rotating power source and blow apart the armor plating to expose the concealed core.

As soon as the core turns red and you announce its impending destruction, face the center of the gate and use your afterburner to speed through. If you hesitate too much, the Prototype Warp Gate will explode, destroying you and Steiner. After the cut-scene, you'll emerge back at the *Mantis* debris field.

Objective: Disable the science vessel's engines and destroy all enemy fighters.

warning

Don't fly too close to the interior of the gate when you're trying to destroy the power source. You'll get pulled back to the *Mantis* debris field and lose the chance to eliminate the Coalition Prototype Warp Gate. Additionally, you won't be able to complete the mission, or its bonus objective, successfully.

Upon returning to the *Mantis* debris field, Command orders you to capture the Coalition science vessel (which entered just as you were pulled into the gate) and disable its engines.

Cycle through enemy targets until you've located the science vessel. Press the subtarget key to cycle through the craft's subsystems. Target its engines and use your afterburner to approach. Follow behind the ship and use your primary weapons, pointed at the targeted engine subsystem, to disable it (see Figure 5.7). Make sure not to destroy the science vessel once its engines are down.

Figure 5.7: Lock on the science vessel's engine subsystem and attack it from close range.

As you did against the Prototype Warp Gate, take on the escort fighters first to eliminate their numbers (but move quickly). Order your wingmen against individual fighters and divert full power to your fighter's shields in preparation for your assault on the larger vessel.

Once the science vessel is disabled and all fighters are destroyed, Klaus Steiner orders you back to the *ANS Reliant*. Open communications with the Alliance base and get permission to land to complete the mission successfully.

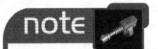

note

Conquering Mission 3 successfully, and with the bonus, requires destroying the Warp Gate and disabling the science vessel's engines. However, you can still successfully complete the mission by destroying the Warp Gate only.

Mission Debriefing

Success plus Bonus: Warp Gate destroyed, science vessel captured, and escorts eliminated.

Success: Warp Gate destroyed, science vessel and escorts escape.

Partial Success: Warp Gate and science vessel destroyed.

 Partial Fail: Warp Gate active, science vessel captured, and escorts destroyed.

 Fail: Warp Gate active, science vessel and escorts escape.

 Fail plus Kick out: Warp Gate active and science vessel destroyed.

Mission 4

Mission Date: August 7, 2160

Briefing: Due to a blind spot in our forward defenses, Intelligence is sending out one of our radar installation squadrons—the Condors—to plug the gap. Our job is to provide fighter cover.

Upon takeoff, you'll rendezvous with the Condors at Nav point 1. A contingent from Alpha will then fly ahead and scout the drop zone while the rest of the wing holds back and provides cover for the Condors. Once the drop zone has been given the all clear, the Condors will move in and begin deploying the single-turreted early warning satellites.

Your primary mission is to keep an eye out for the enemy. If any appear, take them out. Once the satellites are deployed, you will escort the Condors back to Nav point 1 before returning to base.

Ship Selection and Missile Load Out

Protecting the Condors while they deploy the satellites is the most difficult task you've been given thus far. Defeating the swarm of Coalition fighters blitzing the Condors takes speed, missile capacity, and primary weapon firepower. Don't bother with the Predator (though its Blind Fire will prove useful) or the Naginata; both vessels are too light and lack sufficient firepower to deal with the Coalition force.

Take the Grendel, which boasts both the missile capacity and primary weapon abilities to eliminate the Coalition force quickly. Or, if you were able to release the Coyote fighter by scoring a large number of kills in the previous missions, select it instead. The Coyote features the weapon capabilities of the Grendel and the Blind Fire special ability of the Predator. Also, the Coyote has slight speed and mobility advantages over the Grendel.

Outfit the Grendel or Coyote with one or two disrupting Havoc missiles and as many Bandit missiles as your remaining hardpoints can hold. Don't waste any missiles against the first wave of fighters you face; only use them against the Coalition force that directly threatens the Condors. Use the Havocs to disrupt the attack and the Bandits to clean up.

> ## warning
>
> **If you failed to destroy the Coalition Warp Protogate in the previous mission, you'll face a fighter attack as soon as Mission 4 begins. Target the attack force quickly and keep them away from the Condors.**

Battle Plan

Objective: Rendezvous with and escort the Condors.

The mission begins at the *Reliant*. Once ordered, jump to the next Nav point to stay ahead of the Condors and clear the area. You'll discover no Coalition forces at the Nav point and the Condors will warp in as soon as they're given the go-ahead from headquarters.

Sierra Delta, an Alliance convoy, jumps in soon after to alert the Condors to the presence of Coalition signals at the next Nav point. Alliance Command orders you to the next Nav point to clear the zone of any Coalition hunting packs.

Objective: Clear drop zone of any enemy activity.

Jump to the next mission area after receiving the warning from the Sierra Delta convoy. Moments after you arrive, a wing of three Haidar and three Karak Coalition fighters will enter to attack. Thankfully, the Condors remain at the previous Nav point, so you don't need to protect them during this first assault. Eliminate the small Coalition force with primary weapons, saving as many missiles as possible for use against the next two waves of more difficult adversaries.

Once you've cleared the drop zone, the Condors warp in and announce the deployment of the satellites. Target the vessels as soon as they enter the mission area. Point your fighter in their direction and use your afterburner to reach them as soon as possible (see Figure 5.8). Watch the cut-scene of the Condors releasing the satellites and prepare for battle—a difficult Coalition attack follows within seconds.

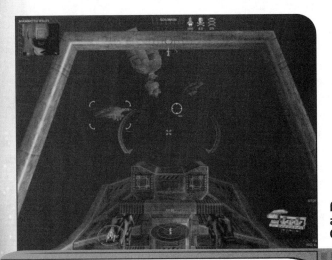

Figure 5.8: Target the Condors and stay close when the Coalition forces attack.

Objective: Protect the Condors while they deploy the satellites.

Just seconds after the Condors begin satellite deployment, eight Coalition fighters (a mixture of Haidar and Karak-class ships) enter and attack. Press the target-nearest-enemy button as soon as you gain control after the brief cut-scene. Use the target direction indicator arrow positioned around your crosshair to locate the Coalition force.

As soon as you face the Coalition fighters (spot the red targeting reticle), lock and launch your Havoc warhead. The resulting explosion will disrupt the advancing fighters and buy you some time to knock them out. Order wingmen to attack specific ships, but don't do so in neglect any of your current targets. Saving the first Condor is extremely difficult and takes speed and quick kills. Selecting a fighter with ample primary weaponry (the Grendel works best) and Blind Fire ability (the Coyote), combined with ample missiles, offer the best chance of saving all Condor ships. Use all your Bandit missiles if you're struggling against the Coalition attack force. Protecting the Condors here is much more important than the objective you'll face at the end of the mission.

note

Don't worry about taking out Nicolai Petrov's Black Guard fighter. He'll launch some Solomon missiles, cloak, taunt the Allied forces, order a Coalition torpedo bomber in, and jump out of the mission area before you even have a chance to engage him.

Objective: Investigate distress call.

With the second wave of Coalition fighters destroyed, the Condors complete deployment and warp out of the mission area. Enriquez announces that the Sierra Delta convoy, the same convoy you met up with earlier in the mission, has sent off a distress call. When prompted, jump to the next mission area and respond.

Upon entering the next zone, you'll notice that just a single Mammoth ship, the *Larson's Pride*, remains from the Sierra Delta convoy. As you approach, Nicolai Petrov and a squadron of Black Guard Basilisk fighters de-cloak and ambush your wing. Prepare to use missile decoys as soon as the ambush begins; the Black Guard fighters launch several volleys of fire-and-forget missiles and many lock onto your own ship.

Objective: Destroy Coalition Black Guard fighters.

Target and engage the Black Guard fighters. Use your remaining locking missiles on their crafts. If possible, however, save a few for use against a torpedo bomber that enters the area shortly after the Black Guard fighters. You might need them to take out its threatening payload.

Listen for Nicolai Petrov to order the Coalition torpedo bomber against the Mammoth ship (see Figure 5.9). Ignore the remaining Black Guard fighters and cycle through enemy targets until you locate the bomber, then ignite your afterburner and quickly intercept it. Fire off any remaining missiles against the bomber or save them for use against any launched torpedoes.

Saving the Mammoth ship fulfills the second part of the mission's bonus objective. Concentrate on any launched torpedoes and eliminate them by using locking missiles or primary weapons. Match speed with the torpedoes if you get too close because if you ram the Coalition bombs you'll be destroyed instantly and have to replay the mission.

Enriquez will order you back to the *Reliant* once you've cleared the final mission area of Coalition forces. Jump back to the capital ship and use the communication display to land and end the mission.

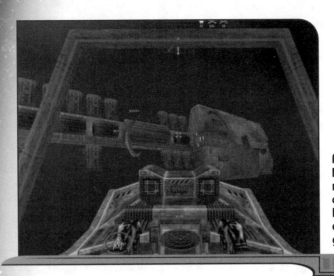

Figure 5.9: Protecting the Mammoth ship requires eliminating several torpedoes. Stick close to the Mammoth and knock out the torpedoes with either locking missiles or your guns.

Mission Debriefing

 Success plus Bonus: All Condors and Mammoths survive.

 Success: All Condors survive.

 Partial Success: One or two Condors destroyed.

 Fail: More than two Condors destroyed.

Mission 5

Mission Date: August 15, 2160

Briefing: As you know, the Alliance is hanging on by a thread. The Coalition have us cornered and supplies are running critically low. Due to our situation, Command has ordered several fully laden Mammoth carriers, that were trapped behind enemy lines, to assemble and prepare to make a run for Alliance territory.

Because of the long-range nature of this mission, the *Reliant* will not be available for backup as her presence would arouse too much Coalition interest. Therefore, you are on your own.

Upon rendezvous at Nav point 3, you will take up escort positions and provide fighter cover up to the Alliance forward line where you will be relieved at Fort Sherman.

Ship Selection and Missile Load Out

Rescuing the Alliance Mammoth carriers is only one component of this varied mission. To complement the mission's diversity, you'll need an equally well-equipped ship, one that features both ample speed and firepower. Don't dismiss the Predator and Naginata; their speed and mobility (and the Predator's Blind Fire) make them excellent torpedo- and bomber-interception craft.

The Predator and Naginata, while moderately effective, will provide the greatest challenge. For an easier mission, select either the Grendel or Crusader (or the Coyote if you can access it at this point) for their added guns, missile hardpoints, and durability over the smaller ships.

Outfit the missile hardpoints with a majority of Bandit locking missiles. They'll come in handy against the torpedo bomber and its payload, and against the Coalition fighters. Equip Screamer pods or Jackhammer missiles on the remaining hardpoints for use against the freighter's subsystems.

Battle Plan

Objective: Rendezvous with the convoy.

After leaving the Reliant, you'll learn that Colonel McGann and the Special Forces unit, the Cobras, will be helping to clear a path for the Mammoth convoy you're protecting. When given the order, press the jump-drive button to proceed to the next mission area . . . where you'll emerge right in the middle of a battle between the Coalition and the Cobras. Several Coalition fighters are escorting the Badanov cruiser. Immediately target the nearest Coalition fighter and attack. Don't bother assaulting the Badanov; as you enter, the Cobras are already hard at work on the vessel's shield generators. It won't be long before the damage exposes the Badanov's hull to a volley of Gamma wing's torpedoes.

Assist in destroying the fighter escort and listen for Colonel McGann to call for Gamma wing to torpedo the Badanov as soon as its shields go down. The Badanov will explode in a magnificent fireball display. Continue to eliminate any remaining escort fighters and listen for orders from Alliance Command and Colonel McGann, who, along with the Cobras, will head out to their next mission. As soon as you're prompted, jump to the next Nav point.

Objective: Destroy cargo ship shield generator.

Though the zone will appear quiet as you enter, a Coalition force—consisting of a cargo freighter, a Kurgen, and fighter escort—soon emerges. While your original objective was to rendezvous with the Alliance convoy, Enriquez appears on the communication display and orders you to make an assault on the Coalition convoy. She specifically tells you to disable the freighter, and soon calls the Cobras back to assist.

Don't bother with the fighter escort or the Kurgen. Cycle through targets until you've got the freighter on the target display. Press the sub-target key until you bring up the shield generator. Locate the freighter on the viewscreen and approach it. You'll notice the shield generator is highlighted in red (see Figure 5.10). Fire your primary weapons on the generator; don't waste missiles here as it won't take many shots to knock it out.

tip

If the freighter's fighter escort targets you, peel off your attack on the cargo ship and concentrate on the fighters until the specific ship is destroyed. Alternatively, you can order your wingmen to attack specific Coalition fighters to keep them off your tail.

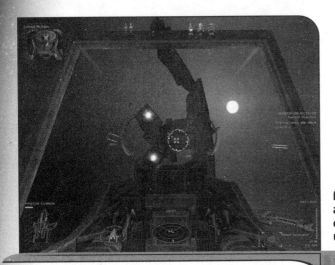

Figure 5.10: With the freighter and shield generator targeted, disable the cargo ship's shields with your primary weapons.

Objective: Destroy cargo ship engines.

Once the shield generator ignites in a ball of flame, Enriquez orders your wing to target and destroy the freighter's engines to keep it from escaping. Cycle through the freighter's subtargets until you've selected its engines. Approach the freighter from the rear and match speed. Use your guns and pummel its engines until they're destroyed and the freighter is immobilized.

Colonel McGann orders the Rippers in as soon as the freighter's engines are disabled. An Alliance Mammoth ship is sent in to steal the Coalition freighter's cargo. Clear out any remaining Coalition forces and wait for Enriquez to deliver additional orders. She notifies your wing that the Alliance convoy you were to protect is currently under attack. Jump to the next mission area as soon as you're able to activate the jump drive.

Objective: Escort and protect the convoy from enemy attack.

As indicated by Enriquez's distressing tone, the Alliance convoy, consisting of the Mammoths Sierra Madre, Britannia, Dawn Chorus, and Mayan Gold, is under attack by four Coalition Sabres when you arrive. Target and engage the nearest enemy fighter. As you battle the four Sabres, the Sierra Madre will perish. Don't fret; there's nothing you could have done to save the vessel.

Three Mammoth ships remain after the destruction of the Sierra Madre. Eliminate the remaining Sabres and fly into the red wire frame escort position above one of the Mammoths. Within moments, a Coalition fleet of nine fighters, one torpedo bomber, and one Kurgen attack.

Order your wingmen against the fighter escort while you target the bomber. If you equipped a Havoc missile, use it against the torpedo bomber or the lead fighter. Ready some locking missiles and use your afterburner to intercept the bomber. As you approach, the vessel will likely have launched several torpedoes. Remain targeted on the bomber itself and launch several locking missiles (see Figure 5.11).

Cycle through enemy targets until you locate the torpedoes. Eliminate them one by one; either match speed or slow down significantly so you don't ram into the bombs. Use any remaining locking missiles against the torpedoes to prevent them from impacting against the Mammoth ships. Complete

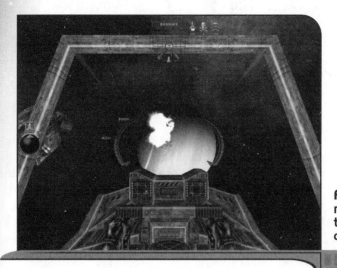

Figure 5.11: Fire a volley of missiles at the torpedo bomber, then concentrate on the torpedoes.

success in the mission requires keeping all Mammoth vessels intact.

With the bomber and torpedo threat out of the way, turn your attention to the remaining Coalition fighters and the Kurgen. Tackle the Kurgen, a moderately-armed corvette, by assigning several wingmen to attack it. Don't let the Kurgen focus only on your vessel. Switch on your ship's ECM to assist in avoiding its laser turrets. It's a small, fairly maneuverable ship, but its armor shouldn't last long against consistent pummeling from your guns. Once the zone is clear, you'll be ordered back to the *Reliant* to land and complete the mission.

tip

Don't hesitate to fire off your remaining missiles against the torpedo bomber and its payload. They're by far the biggest threat to the convoy. The remaining Coalition force can be mopped up with primary weapons.

Mission Debriefing

Success: No Mammoths destroyed.

Partial Success: One Mammoth destroyed.

Partial Failure: Two Mammoths destroyed.

Fail: Three Mammoths destroyed.

Mission 6

Mission Date: August 26, 2160

Briefing: I'm sure you are all aware of the loss of Brad Callen, or "Viper," during our last mission. His jump drive malfunctioned, destroying his fighter. Search and rescue have not found an escape pod. As of now, Mark Bannister, callsign "Bandit," will be taking over as squadron leader.

At 1600 hours we received a distress call from an inbound convoy en route to Triton Command. Reports are sketchy, but we think the convoy consists of a number of fully laden cargo carriers, and more importantly the *ANS Ulysses*, a commandeered civilian liner transporting high-ranking military and Senate personnel.

The convoy has been under constant attack. They've lost their fighter cover and sustained heavy damage. Your first objective will be to link up with the *Ulysses* and the heavy cargo carriers. Once there, escort them to Fort Baxter where you will be relieved and the convoy will undergo repairs and resupply.

Ship Selection and Missile Load Out

Saving the *Ulysses* from four cloaked torpedo bombers, and several other torpedoes, is one of the toughest objectives you've tackled thus far. Protecting the *Ulysses* hinges on your ability to quickly cycle through available targets and avoid enemy fighter fire as you pick off torpedo after torpedo. All other mission objectives pale in comparison.

The Coyote, with its ample missile hardpoints and Blind Fire ability, provides the best chance for success. If you don't have access to the Coyote, the Grendel works nearly as well. The Grendel has an equal amount of missile hardpoints and its primary weapons are powerful. However, the Coyote's Blind Fire special ability makes torpedo interception easier, as does plenty of hardpoints for locking missiles.

Equip your ship with Bandit missiles for use against fighters, but also include a few Havoc missiles to disrupt the several torpedo bombers you'll engage.

Battle Plan

Objective: Protect the *Ulysses* from torpedo fire.

Alliance Command orders you to activate jump drive systems quickly and a fellow wingman shouts over the communication system that this one's for Viper. As soon as you can jump to the next Nav point, press the jump-drive key. You'll emerge with the *Ulysses* and its convoy of four Mammoths and one Prowler about 500 meters away.

tip

When you regain control after the first cut-scene of the torpedo bombers cloaking, target the nearest Basilisk and order a wingman to attack. If you have time, cycle to the next Basilisk and do the same. Repeat again if you're fast enough with the communication display. Your wingmen will keep the Basilisks off your back as you eliminate the bombers and the torpedoes.

Don't hesitate in rendezvousing with the *Ulysses*; the Coalition attacks from the ship's rear, meaning you start the mission at the farthest point from their entrance. Divert additional power to the engines or use your afterburner to reach the vessels as soon as possible. Meanwhile, your wingmen and the *Ulysses* captain will remind you of your primary mission—stopping the torpedoes from impacting on the *Ulysses* or the convoy.

Not long after you reach the *Ulysses*, a Coalition force of four torpedo bombers and two Basilisk fighters emerges from behind the convoy. To make matters even worse, all Coalition ships, including the torpedo bombers, possess the ability to cloak.

Watch two cut-scenes—one of the torpedo bombers cloaking and another of them launching torpedoes—then cycle through enemy targets until you've targeted a bomber. Get it in your crosshairs and select a Havoc missile, then fire off the disrupting warhead to knock out the bomber's electronic systems. Match speed with the damaged vessel and finish it off with primary weapons (see Figure 5.12).

Figure 5.12: Knocking out a torpedo bomber immediately will make your job much easier.

Even though there are torpedoes locked on to the *Ulysses* and its convoy, you should attempt to eliminate one or more of the torpedo bombers at the first opportunity. Your initial attack on the bombers is critical. You need to knock out the closest torpedo bombers, but don't waste so much time that you neglect its launched torpedoes. Count off seven seconds after you begin the attack on the first bomber. As soon as you hit the time limit, change target to the torpedoes.

What makes the protection of the *Ulysses* and its convoy so difficult is that the torpedo bombers cloak periodically after launching three

warning

Saving the *Ulysses* is the most important task in this mission, as its survival or destruction has the most effect on the mission's future branching and success. However, losing any member of the convoy will prevent you from completing the mission's bonus objective.

or four torpedoes. During this time, you won't be able to target them. However, you can use Havoc missiles from a distance to prevent them from cloaking and firing. If you've got a lock, though, one or two Bandit missiles should finish it off. Remember that additional volleys of torpedoes will be launched at the convoy as long as the bombers remain in the mission area—destroying the bombers means fewer torpedoes. Just because you can't target the bombers doesn't mean they're not there. They're likely cloaked, so keep cycling through targets until they become available.

Continue to divide time between eliminating torpedoes (highest priority) and targeting the torpedo bombers. Once you've targeted a bomber, don't waste time trying to reach it and use your primary weapons; select a locking missile and blow the enemy ship apart from a distance. Destroy the torpedoes by cycling through targets until you've selected one, then match its speed and either fire on it with your guns or launch a locking missile.

Your next mission objective depends on whether or not the *Ulysses* survived the attack. If you saved the *Ulysses*, skip down to the "Protect the Rippers" objective of this mission walkthrough. If several torpedoes impacted against the vessel's hull, the captain announces the launch of escape pods and you must continue on to the objective below, "Protect the Nanny."

Objective: Protect the Nanny (if you failed to save the *Ulysses* from torpedo attack). Alliance Command orders a Nanny ship to enter the area and pick up the escape pods. All Coalition ships jump out after the destruction of the *Ulysses*, so the Nanny initially jumps into an enemy-free zone. Locate the pickup ship by cycling through friendly targets. Moments after the Nanny ship enters, a Coalition Antonov pickup ship enters with eight Saracen fighters. If the Coalition fighters destroy the Nanny ship, Allied Command orders you to take out the remaining life pods so they can't fall into enemy hands. If the Antonov escapes with three pods, the mission is flagged as a failure.

> **tip**
>
> Target the launched torpedoes as you approach the bomber and fire locking missiles. With missiles tracked on the torpedoes, you can ignore them and cycle through the other enemy targets until you select the bomber.

Objective: Destroy the Antonov.
To complicate matters, an Antonov pickup ship arrives to collect the *Ulysses'* escape pods, shortly followed by eight Saracen fighters. Immediately target the Antonov and use your afterburner to approach. Match its speed and pummel the ship's hull with any remaining missiles and your primary weapons (see Figure 5.13).

Ignore the Coalition fighters and concentrate first on the Antonov, which plans to swipe three escape pods then flee from the scene. The Antonov can't take much punishment. A few missiles and a steady stream of gunfire will destroy the vessel in a matter of seconds.

With the Antonov out of the way, return your attention to the Saracen fighters. They're not much of a threat to the Nanny ship, but you'll still want to work through them as quickly as possible. Save a few locking missiles for the final task—eliminating a Coalition torpedo bomber that's entered and targeted the Nanny.

As soon as you witness the cut-scene of the bomber entering, cycle through enemy targets until you've locked on to the torpedo bomber. Use your afterburner to quickly approach and lock on

Figure 5.13: Make the Antonov your first priority; target it and let your wingmen take on the Saracen escort.

remaining missiles. The bomber will likely have launched a strike on the Nanny by the time you approach, meaning that you might want to concentrate on the torpedoes first.

Rescuing the escape pods has several different outcomes. Saving the Nanny ship and destroying the Antonov provides the best results and a partially successful mission. However, if you fail to protect the Nanny and allow the Antonov to escape with three life pods, the mission is flagged as a failure. If you destroy the Antonov before it escapes (and the Nanny is destroyed), it's a partial failure.

Regardless of the outcome, Alliance Command orders you to return to Fort Baxter and then to the *Reliant* in order to complete the mission.

Objective: Protect the Rippers (if you saved the *Ulysses* from torpedo attack). Saving the *Ulysses* allows you to escort the vessel to Fort Baxter. Press the jump-drive key when ordered to the Alliance base. When you arrive, Alliance Command notifies you that an arms freighter is under Coalition attack and to head there immediately. Activate your jump drive when prompted.

Unfortunately, the Allied arms freighter explodes the moment you arrive. However, the

tip

Try not to venture too far from the cargo pods and keep an eye on any Coalition fighters not engaged by either you or your wingmen. Any Coalition fighter not occupied is one that could target the Rippers.

valuable cargo has been jettisoned and remains intact. Several wings of Coalition Sabre, Azan, and Kossac fighters remain in the mission area. Order your wingmen against specific enemy craft while you target the nearest enemy and engage. As you fight, four Alliance Ripper ships arrive to collect the valuable cargo (see Figure 5.14).

In order to complete the mission's bonus objective, you must keep each Ripper ship intact. Work quickly through the enemy fighters using as many locking missiles as you have left. Order your wing-

Figure 5.14: Each Ripper collects a separate cargo pod.

men to either attack specific Coalition fighters, or command them to protect the Ripper ships once they've arrived.

Once the Coalition attackers are destroyed, you'll be sent back to the *Reliant* to complete the mission. Press your jump-drive key when ordered, then use the communication display to request landing on the Alliance Command ship.

Mission Debriefing

Success plus Bonus: *Ulysses* survives, all convoy ships intact, and all Rippers survive.

Success: *Ulysses* survives with some or none of its convoy intact.

Partial Success: *Ulysses* destroyed, Nanny survives, Antonov destroyed.

Partial Failure: *Ulysses*, Nanny, and Antonov destroyed.

Fail: *Ulysses* destroyed, Nanny destroyed, and Antonov escapes.

Mission 7

Mission Date: September 22, 2160

Briefing: Intelligence reports have confirmed that the *CS Rameses*, a Russian carrier, is currently en route to rendezvous with an incoming Coalition battle group. We believe she is shy on fighter support, leaving her open for attack.

Our first objective will be to intercept the *Rameses* and eliminate any remaining fighters. Secondly, we will need to get up close and take out her flak turrets. With the *Rameses'* defenses neutralized, Gamma wing can start their torpedo run.

We must strike quickly; if we take too long we will have an incoming Coalition battle group crashing our party. If all goes to plan, we'll have a Coalition carrier scalp to add to the kill board, but remember to stick to the game plan and pay attention to your communication display.

Ship Selection and Missile Load Out

Note

Saving the Fort Baxter escape pods has no effect on the mission's final outcome. The only difference is that if you eliminate all Coalition fighters with escape pods remaining, Ronin wing enters to supervise the Nanny ship. If you lose all the escape pods, you're simply ordered to the attack on the *Rameses* and Ronin wing stays home.

Dogfighting the abundant *Rameses* Saracen escort provides this mission's biggest challenge. To compensate, you'll need a tough fighter with ample primary weaponry and plenty of afterburner fuel to keep up with the elusive enemy craft. Selecting a fighter with an extended ECM or Spectral Shields also helps during your attack on the *Rameses*.

The Coyote, Crusader, and Grendel will all prove effective, though the Coyote has an edge thanks to its Blind Fire special ability. The Spectral Shields of the Crusader also adds extra defenses against the plentiful Coalition fighters and the turrets of the *Rameses*. All three vessels are agile enough to keep up with the Saracen fighters and have enough shield strength and armor to withstand significant punishment.

Outfit your hardpoints with Bandit missiles for use against the Saracen fighters. In order to quickly eliminate the *Rameses*' shield generator, you may wish to equip one or two powerful Jackhammer missiles. Alternatively, you can load a pod of Screamer missiles, since the target is nearly stationary.

Battle Plan

Objective: Hunt down the *Rameses* and the Saracen fighters. Go to the aid of Fort Baxter. After your ship launches from the *Reliant*, Alliance Command realizes that the *Rameses* isn't at its expected position. Instead, the Coalition carrier is currently attacking the Alliance base, Fort Baxter. Command orders you to immediately jump to Fort Baxter and help defend it. When prompted, initiate your jump drive by pressing the defined key.

However, your efforts will be in vain as Fort Baxter succumbs to the torpedo barrage of the *Rameses* as soon as you enter the mission area. Target the *Rameses* and head in its direction. As you approach, fellow wingmen and Alliance

Note

Though there's no time limit, you should destroy the escort force as quickly as possible as the *Reliant* is taking a pounding from the *Rameses*' laser turrets. Also, the order to attack the *Rameses*' shield generator only comes after you've eliminated the escort force.

Command announce that life pods have jettisoned from Fort Baxter. Nanny pickup ships are on the way and your new orders are to protect them while they collect the escape pods.

Objective: Protect the escape pods and await the Nanny pickup ships.

Continue moving toward the *Rameses* and cycling through enemy targets. You'll eventually be able to select the Saracen and Sabre fighters that launch from the carrier to destroy the escape pods (see Figure 5.15). Ignore the *Rameses*, as it jumps out of the area in a matter of moments. Instead, head for the nearest Coalition fighter and engage it.

warning

Fail to destroy the *Rameses* here and you'll encounter the Coalition carrier, as well as Al-Rahan and a squadron of Saracen fighters, again in Mission 20.

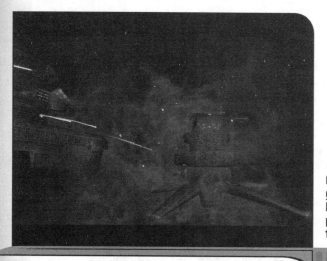

Figure 5.15: There's nothing you can do to save Fort Baxter. But you can save the escape pods by engaging the Coalition fighters quickly.

Work quickly through the Saracen and Sabre fighters, but save as many of your missiles as possible for the next objective. Order your wingmen to attack specific fighters and stay close to the Nanny ships in order to engage any Coalition fighter going after the escape pods. Once you've cleared the area, you'll be ordered to jump after the *Rameses*, which is currently assaulting the *Reliant*.

Objective: Hunt down the *Rameses* and the Saracen fighters.

The *Reliant* and *Rameses* are already engaged as you enter the next mission area. Furthermore, over a dozen Saracen fighters are protecting the *Rameses* and assisting with the attack on the *Reliant*. Use your afterburner to quickly reach the heart of the Saracen fighters. As you approach, a Coalition ace named Al-Rahan taunts you over the communication system. If you engage Al-Rahan, he'll evacuate the mission area once his ship has sustained significant damage. Letting him hang around, though, adds a difficult adversary to the mission area. Consider engaging him immediately, or send several wingmen to attack his fighter while you engage the other Saracen fighters. Concentrate solely on the Saracen escort and don't bother assaulting the *Rameses*. Try to stay away from the Coalition carrier if possible, only venturing near if your dogfight with the Saracen fighters takes you there. Activate your fighter's ECM if you fly around the *Rameses* to add some protection against its powerful laser turrets. Continue to cycle through Saracen fighters and keep your wingmen occupied by ordering them against specific opponents. Once you've eliminated the escorts, Captain Foster orders you to attack the *Rameses'* shield generator.

Objective: Take out the shield generator on the *Rameses*.

Target the *Rameses* and use the cycle through subtargets key to locate its shield generator. Approaching the *Rameses* isn't easy; a few hits from its plentiful laser turrets will knock out your fighter's shields and armor in a matter of seconds. Divert additional power to the shields and switch on your ECM for more protection against the Command vessel's anti-fighter systems (see Figure 5.16).

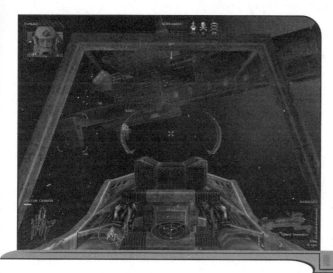

Figure 5.16: Protect your fighter with additional shield power and its ECM while approaching the *Rameses*.

Directly approach the shield generator and use locking missiles—especially the powerful Jackhammers—to eliminate it quickly. Order wingmen against the shield generator for further assistance. If you start to lose forward shields and armor, turn away from the *Rameses* and wait until your shields are restored before resuming the attack run.

Objective: Protect Gamma wing.

With the *Rameses'* shield generator destroyed, Captain Foster orders Gamma wing, a squad of Alliance torpedo bombers, to assault the vulnerable Coalition carrier. To protect itself, the *Rameses* launches another wing of Saracen fighters. Engage the Saracen squadron as soon as it enters the mission area and keep them away from Gamma wing.

You can lose one bomber from Gamma wing and still destroy the *Rameses*. Don't give up if you hear that a Gamma wing bomber has been destroyed. Keep attacking the Saracen fighters!

Keeping Gamma wing alive and attacking the *Rameses* will ensure the carrier's destruction—and a successful mission. Once the *Rameses* explodes, clear out the remaining Coalition fighters. Use the communication system to ask the *Reliant* for permission to land.

If Gamma wing fails in its mission to destroy the *Rameses,* you'll need to engage the carrier to keep it away from the *Reliant*. Swoop close to the Coalition carrier and engage its laser turrets. Divert power to your shields and initiate your ECM to protect yourself against its lasers. Should the *Reliant* jump out, you'll follow and land on the Alliance Command ship safely (though the mission will be flagged a failure). If the *Rameses* destroys the *Reliant*, you'll jump to the *Yamato*, land in its hangar, and promptly be kicked out of the Alliance military for the huge mission failure.

Mission Debriefing

Success: *Rameses* destroyed.

Fail: Gamma wing destroyed and *Reliant* escapes.

Fail plus Kick out: Gamma wing and *Reliant* destroyed.

chapter 6

Raiders: The Guerrilla War—
Missions 8 to 11

With seven missions notched on their belt, the 45th Volunteers can hardly be referred to as rookies any longer. While the war with the Coalition is still an uphill battle, several key victories in the first campaign have paved the way for larger offensives. Unfortunately for the Alliance, though, a traitor may be in their midst.

In this chapter you'll find comprehensive walkthroughs covering the next four missions that comprise the second campaign of *StarLancer*. Lessons learned from the success and failure of your first sorties will serve you well here. While you'll engage plenty of Coalition fighters and have to intercept several torpedo runs, the second campaign is characterized by several attacks on Coalition capital ships and bases. Be prepared for a tough fight against difficult odds!

Mission 8

Mission Date: October 30, 2160
Briefing: We have received orders from HQ to go directly to Fort Carter for repairs and resupply. At our current speed, we should make our destination by 2200 hours. Proceed with caution as our route takes us through areas of reported Coalition activity.

In order to be safe, you will be riding in front of and behind the *Reliant*—just in case we encounter any unwelcome guests. We are vulnerable to attack and need those repairs. A couple of torpedoes could take us out, so make sure you stay alert!

Ship Selection and Missile Load Out

This mission requires a ship with the speed to intercept multiple torpedo launches and the durability to survive a close encounter with the laser turrets of the Coalition carrier *Krasnaya*. Unfortunately, you won't be able to select a ship with the optimum ability in both categories.

Select a ship based on your struggles thus far. If you've had trouble intercepting torpedoes, select a faster ship with plenty of afterburner fuel. If you're adept at intercepting torpedoes, but have problems keeping your ship intact against laser and missile fire, then choose a more durable ship with higher ECM and Spectral Shields.

The Coyote (if you've accessed the ship by this point, of course) strikes the best balance. Its Blind Fire ability provides an easier primary weapon attack against the torpedoes and its plentiful ECM and decent armor class protect you against the *Krasnaya*'s armaments. Select the Grendel if you value toughness and the best selection of primary guns. The Grendel's main drawback is its lack of afterburner fuel, though this problem can be solved by selecting a fuel pod during missile load out. Another option is the Naginata. Its speed and afterburner fuel quantity make it the best torpedo interceptor, and its Spectral Shields and ample ECM should protect you and the Naginata's poor armor class.

Intercepting torpedoes takes many seconds of afterburner fuel, so don't hesitate to arm a fuel pod on one or two of the missile hardpoints. Load up the remainder of hardpoints with Bandit missiles for use against torpedoes and fighters.

Battle Plan

Objective: Escort *Reliant* to Fort Carter. Protect the *Reliant* from attack.
You'll take up escort position just in front of the *Reliant* on its way to Fort Carter. Unfortunately, the trip is rather brief as a huge Coalition carrier, the *Krasnaya*, emerges almost immediately from a Warp Gate, launches fighters, and attacks the *Reliant*.

Immediately target the nearest Coalition Sabre and engage it. Don't use any of your locking missiles against the Sabres; you shouldn't have much trouble eliminating the light Coalition vessels with primary weapons only. As you battle the fighters, Enriquez announces that the *Krasnaya* has launched torpedoes against the *Reliant*. She then orders you to ignore these torpedoes as the *Reliant*'s laser turrets will handle them. Continue battling the fighters until Enriquez announces the destruction of all launched torpedo warheads (see Figure 6.1).

Figure 6.1: The *Krasnaya* launches torpedoes at the *Reliant*. Enriquez has it covered, though, so continue battling the fighter escort.

Once all of the *Krasnaya*'s torpedoes are eliminated by the *Reliant*, Enriquez announces the presence of three Coalition Kamov torpedo bombers that have warped into a triangular position around the *Reliant*. Within moments, the bombers begin firing torpedoes at the *Reliant*.

As soon as the bombers arrive, ignore the Coalition fighters and return to the *Reliant*. Stick close to the Alliance Command ship and blow apart the torpedoes as they close on the vessel's position. Save locking missiles for use against the torpedoes. Selecting a fighter with Blind Fire ability makes destroying the torpedoes and defending the *Reliant* much easier.

Order your wingmen to engage specific torpedoes to help the cause. You can also order wingmen to take on the bombers, but don't go after the bombers yourself. In order to keep all torpedoes off the *Reliant* (and achieve the mission's bonus objective), you must stick close to the ship in order to have a shot at each warhead.

tip

You don't need to destroy the bombers. After they launch around four warheads each, they'll jump out of the mission area. Because the bombers are positioned so far away from the *Reliant*, it's too difficult to afterburn your way to their position; destroy them, and return to the *Reliant* in time to keep the torpedoes off its hull. Instead, stick close to the *Reliant* and hit the torpedoes as they come in.

If four torpedoes hit the *Reliant*, the Alliance Command ship will be destroyed. You'll be forced to land on the *Yamato*, and the mission will end in a failure. Furthermore, you'll have to perform the mission again.

Objective: Destroy the *Krasnaya's* shield generator.

Once the Kamov bombers have been destroyed or have exited the mission area, Klaus Steiner orders the 45th to attack the *Krasnaya*'s shield generator in hopes of bringing in a Gamma wing of bombers to destroy the Coalition carrier. Cycle through enemy targets until you've selected the *Krasnaya* and use the subtarget key to locate its shield generator.

As with all subtargets, you'll be able to pick out the shield generator from its red highlights. Approach the *Krasnaya*, avoiding its laser turret fire, both with an activated ECM and with additional power diverted to your shields. Destroy the shield generator with a barrage of primary weapon fire or by using any remaining missiles.

Objective: Disable the *Krasnaya's* defenses.

With the shield down, Steiner orders the 45th to further weaken the *Krasnaya* by taking out its plentiful laser turrets. Gamma wing's torpedoes won't stand a chance against the Coalition ship unless these weapons are neutralized. Target the *Krasnaya* and use the subtarget key to cycle through the laser turrets. Don't bother to wait until you've targeted the laser turret to blow it apart. If you see a laser turret as you're flying around the *Krasnaya*, take it out with primary weapons, then move on to your next target.

Knocking out the laser turrets takes a wide variety of skills (see Figure 6.2). You must keep your ECM as active as possible to defend yourself against the laser blasts, you'll need to keep full power diverted to the shields at all times, and you must balance the shields in case one side gets blown off by the turrets.

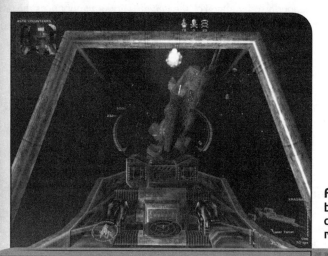

Figure 6.2: Keep your shields balanced and ECM active while destroying the *Krasnaya's* turret defenses.

The easiest way to maneuver around the *Krasnaya* is to target the laser turrets and match speed, in effect reducing your velocity to zero. Move to each new laser turret target using either small bursts of afterburner or by lightly accelerating on the throttle. Order your wingmen to assist against the turrets, but don't rely on them to work as quickly as you do.

Objective: Destroy all remaining fighters.

Disabling the laser turrets cues the arrival of Gamma wing and its torpedo run against the *Krasnaya*. At this time, Steiner orders the 45th to engage the remaining Coalition fighters. Order your wingmen to take on specific enemy fighters while you target and attack the nearest Sabre. Be sure to use any remaining locking missiles against the remaining fighter force, as this is the mission's final objective.

Though the most difficult portion of the episode is over, don't neglect your duty to eliminate the remaining fighters. If the Coalition ships manage to take down Gamma wing, the *Krasnaya* will escape and the mission will end in a partial failure.

With the *Krasnaya* destroyed (or escaped), Enriquez orders you to jump to the next mission area and Fort Carter. Once there, conclude the mission by using the communication display to request permission to land.

warning

Once the order comes through, you must knock out the *Krasnaya*'s laser turrets quickly. If you're too slow, the Coalition, realizing imminent doom, activates the vessel's jump engines and exits the mission area. If the *Krasnaya* escapes, the mission ends with a partial failure.

Mission Debriefing

Success plus Bonus: *Krasnaya* destroyed and no torpedo hits on *Reliant*.

Success: *Krasnaya* destroyed and one torpedo hit on *Reliant*.

Partial Success: *Krasnaya* destroyed and two or three torpedo hits on *Reliant*.

Partial Fail: *Krasnaya* escapes.

Fail plus Kick out: *Reliant* destroyed by four torpedo hits.

Mission 9

Mission Date: November 13, 2160

Briefing: We've received reports of a large Coalition strike force headed our way. A Command ship and escort carriers support them. Headquarters has teamed us up with the *ANS Endeavor* and her base squadron, the Hellcats, so we are in good company.

The key objective will be to attack the Coalition class two carrier. Once the carrier is engaged, the Marine boarding craft will hit the Command ship where we hope to obtain vital data about enemy movements. Lt. Commander Stahl will be joining the Marine boarding party. His knowledge of Coalition craft and systems should prove useful.

Your objectives are as follows. The *Reliant*, *Endeavor*, and Hellcats will engage the carrier group while Alpha wing will proceed to the rear of the convoy and disable the Command ship and its escort allowing the boarding ship to move in and dock. Once the Marines get onto the Command ship, the boarding craft will disengage and wait for the pick up signal. After pick up, rendezvous with the *Reliant* at the prearranged Nav point.

If all goes according to plan, we will gain valuable information, which will help reinforce our position in this quadrant.

Ship Selection and Missile Load Out

An attack on two Coalition capital ships demands a tough ship with plenty of primary weapons. You'll face a few waves of fighters in the mission, but eliminating the numerous laser turrets on the Berijev and the well-armed Kurgen require the most attention.

Select either the Crusader or the Grendel. Both are extremely durable, with high armor class and shield rating, and carry a respectable number of primary weapons and missile hardpoints. Though it features slightly less firepower, the Crusader's Spectral Shields and extra second of afterburner fuel should assist you during the mission.

Equip your ship's missile hardpoints with Bandit missiles that will help you protect the boarding ship from Coalition fighters. Outfit a few Havoc missiles to disrupt their electronic systems and buy some extra time if the boarding ship comes under attack.

warning

If you're concentrating on the Coalition fighters and a 45th wingman recommends you hurry up against the Berijev, immediately turn your attention to the Coalition capital ship. It won't be much longer before the Berijev flees the mission area and you'll return to the *Reliant* in disgrace.

Battle Plan

Objective: Destroy the Sabres and the Kurgen.

Launch from the *Reliant* and receive the orders to jump into the next mission area. Activate your jump drive when prompted. A cut-scene of the Alliance and Coalition battle will greet you. The Hellcats are currently engaged with a carrier group diverting a large segment of the Coalition defenses. You're ordered to take on the Sabres and the Kurgen defending the Berijev in order to clear a path for an Alliance boarding ship (see Figure 6.3).

Though you should spend some time battling the fighters and Kurgen, don't neglect your initial orders for this mission, which are to disable the Berijev's shield generator, engines, and defenses. If you wait too long, the Berijev will jump out of the mission area and you'll immediately be sent back to the *Reliant* and receive a failure and kick out. Order your wingmen to engage the Sabres and the Kurgen. Eliminate a few, but proceed against the Berijev as soon as possible.

Objective: Destroy the Berijev's shield generator.

Cycle through targets until you've selected the Berijev, then use the subtarget key to locate the shield generator. If you're pressed for time, order some wingmen to assist. Approach the Berijev, which isn't moving very fast, and locate the highlighted section. Divert power to the shields and activate your ECM for extra defenses against the capital ship's laser turrets. Save your locking missiles for later in the mission and use guns against the immobile generator. Remember, although Alliance Command recommends that you destroy the shield generator first, you can take out the Berijev's subtargets in any order. It's highly recommended you go for the engines first. That way, the Berijev won't be able to flee the mission area even if you're taking too long against its other defenses.

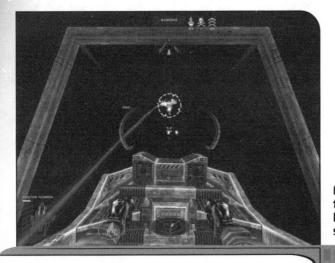

Figure 6.3: Work through the fighter escort quickly. Use a Bandit missile or two if you're struggling.

Objective: Destroy the Berijev's engines. With the shield generator destroyed, Allied Command orders you to fire on the Berijev's engines. It takes two subtargets to disable the Berijev's mobility. Approach the first highlighted area and eliminate it with primary weapons. Move on to the second and blow it apart (see Figure 6.4). Once again, don't concern

tip

While you're occupied with the Berijev, make sure your wingmen are engaged with both the Sabres and the nearby Kurgen. The more fighter defenses eliminated, the greater chance the boarding ship will complete its mission.

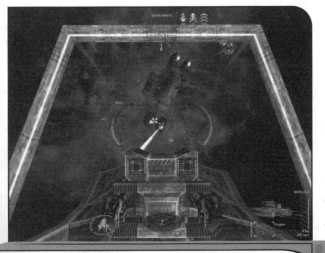

Figure 6.4: The Berijev's engines come in two parts. Don't forget to destroy both or the Berijev might flee the area!

yourself with the Sabre fighters. Order your wingmen to occupy the fighters and give you time to work on the Berijev.

Objective: Destroy the Berijev's defenses.

With the shield generator and engines destroyed, only the Berijev's laser turrets remain; these must now be destroyed in order for the boarding ship to complete its mission. Thankfully, there aren't as many turrets on the Berijev as there were on the *Krasnaya* from the previous mission. Cycle through the Berijev's subtargets to locate the nearest laser turret and engage it. Because you're so close to the turrets, you should divert power to the shields, switch on the ECM, and ready your shield-balance key to protect yourself.

Objective: Protect the boarding ship.

Once you've destroyed the Berijev's shield generator, engines, and laser turrets, Allied Command sends in the boarding ship to dock with the crippled enemy vessel. As the boarding ship makes its way to the Berijev, another wing of Coalition Saracen fighters enters. Stick close to the Berijev and eliminate any nearby Coalition fighters, including the Kurgen if it's still active. Use your locking missiles during your defense of the boarding ship. If you lose it, the 45th is sent to the next Nav point and ordered back to the *Reliant* to face the consequences of a failed mission.

Objective: Destroy the *Kozah's* shield generator.

If the boarding ship completes its mission, you're ordered to assist the Hellcats in their battle with the *Kozah* carrier and its fighter defenses—specifically to eliminate the *Kozah*'s shield generator. Don't hesitate in proceeding toward the *Kozah*; if you take too long to knock out its shields, the vessel will jump out of the mission area and you'll lose the bonus objective opportunity.

Keep any remaining Coalition fighters occupied by ordering your wingmen against them. Cycle through the *Kozah*'s subtargets to locate the shield generator, then approach the highlighted section and eliminate it with primary weapons (see Figure 6.5). As you should against any capital ships, divert power to the shields and switch on your ECM for protection against the turrets. With the shield generator down, Allied Command launches torpedoes to eliminate the carrier. Don't use your remaining missiles against the *Kozah*'s shield generator. You still have one task left to complete after this, so be sure to save some missiles to make that last objective much easier.

note

Colonel McGann aborts his assault on the boarding ship once he takes 40 percent damage to his ship or you eliminate four of his wingmen. If you have several locking missiles left, fire them all at McGann. If not, concentrate on his wingmen since Colonel McGann's fighter provides a difficult dogfighting challenge.

Objective: Protect the boarding ship.

After either you destroy the *Kozah*, or the *Kozah* escapes, Stahl (piloting the boarding ship) calls for assistance from the next mission area. As soon as you're prompted, activate your jump drive to reach

Figure 6.5: The *Kozah*'s shield generator falls quickly to primary weapons.

the boarding ship's position. Upon arrival you'll discover that Colonel McGann, an Alliance officer you worked with in a previous mission, has betrayed the Allies and attacked the boarding ship.

Immediately target the nearest traitor and engage him quickly. Order your wingmen against specific fighters. If you've saved any locking missiles, use them now to defend the boarding ship. Should it fall to McGann and his gang, the mission ends in a failure.

The *Reliant* jumps in once McGann flees the mission area. Request permission to land to complete the mission.

Mission Debriefing

 Success plus Bonus: Boarding ship survives and *Kozah* destroyed.

 Success: Boarding ship survives and *Kozah* escapes.

 Fail plus Kick out: Berijev escapes.

 Fail plus Kick out: Boarding ship destroyed.

Mission 10

Mission Date: November 21, 2160

Briefing: The Coalition's warp capability is giving them a strong advantage as illustrated by their attacks along our frontier. We have to neutralize this quickly so we can gain the upper hand when our own warp technology is operational. Reconnaissance indicates that this jump gate activity is being coordinated from the Latov Asteroid Observation Base, and our mission's primary objective is its destruction.

Alpha and Gamma wing will move out three Nav points and locate the base using scanners. Once found, Alpha wing will have three minutes to destroy the communication tower; after that the jamming from your support craft will be ineffective. Once you have tagged the communication tower, take out the fighters; when the fighters are gone, destroy the base's defensive turrets. Gamma wing will then move in to take out the base's satellite dish.

Your final objective will be to locate and destroy a vent hatch on the surface of the asteroid, then launch one of your Jackhammer missiles into the vent. This should trigger off a chain reaction in the asteroid's internal bunker. With all mission objectives achieved, make your way back to the *Reliant* via Fort Sherman.

Ship Selection and Missile Load Out

The attack on Latov Base, much like the previous mission, requires a hardy ship; extra ECM and Spectral Shields also come in handy. An encounter with a few fighter groups means you should select the most versatile, yet well-armored, ship in the group.

The Crusader and Coyote (if released) should provide the best chance of mission success. The Grendel's durability is hard to pass up, but its poor agility rating could pose problems during the fighter attacks. Select the Coyote if you've gained access to the vessel. While it's not quite as durable as the Crusader (and slightly lacks primary weapons fire), the Coyote's Blind Fire ability and ECM time gives you an advantage in both the fighter and Latov Base attack. The Mirage, if you've released it with an exceptional kill score, also works well. Though the Mirage lacks the missile hardpoints of the Coyote, it features powerful primary weapons, excellent ECM, and the agility to keep up with Coalition fighters.

If you want to make the killing blow against the Latov Base, then be sure to equip at least one Jackhammer missile on a hardpoint. You don't have to, though—a wingman will take out Latov Base if you lack a Jackhammer or miss with your shot. Fill the remainder of your missile hardpoints with Bandit missiles (for the Coalition fighters) and at least one Havoc missile (for the wave of eight fighters that enter at Nav point 2).

> ## warning
>
> **Don't dawdle against the convoy. If you're too slow, the convoy jumps out of the mission area and you'll lose the opportunity for some easy kills. Apart from the missed kills, however, there are no consequences to failing to eliminate the convoy.**

Battle Plan

Objective: Move out to the Latov Base.

Launch from the *Reliant* with two Gamma wing bombers following close behind. When prompted, jump to the next Nav point. You'll spot two Coalition Sabre fighters and a convoy consisting of a troop transport, two cargo ships, and several Kurgens upon arrival. Target the nearest Sabre first and set an intercept course.

The Sabres protect the convoy, and as soon as one of the Coalition fighters is destroyed, the other jumps out of the mission area to alert its comrades. In order to defeat both Sabres, you should order all wingmen against one while you battle the other. As your wingmen fight one of the Sabres, guide your ship to within 100 meters of the other. Prepare your Bandit missiles; as soon as the 45th announces that the Sabre is fleeing the mission area, launch your missiles. Don't worry if one of the Sabres gets away. It doesn't make the rest of the mission any more difficult; it only changes some of the pilot communication at the next Nav point.

Once the Sabres have been destroyed or chased off, turn your attention to the convoy. The troop transport provides the most durable target; order all your wingmen against it while you eliminate the Kurgens and two cargo ships. Keep your wingmen busy; as soon as they've eliminated one of the convoy vessels, order them to engage another target.

Use your Jackhammer missile against a convoy vessel as you'll be able to rearm at the next Nav point. Don't waste all your other locking missiles, however, as you'll face some Coalition fighters in the next area. After destroying the convoy, Allied Command orders the 45th to the next Nav point to rendezvous with a Nanny ship (see Figure 6.6) for refueling and rearming.

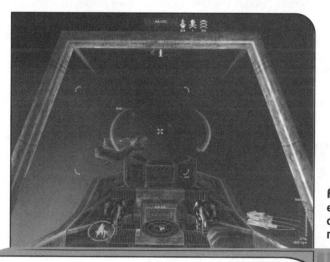

Figure 6.6: Enter the red escort position wire frame to dock with the Nanny ship and rearm and refuel your fighter.

Objective: Protect Gamma.

At the arrival at Nav point 2, you'll find the Nanny ship inexplicably missing. Instead, a Coalition force of four Sabre and four Lagg fighters enters and attacks. Target the nearest fighter and lock on with your Havoc missile (if you equipped one). The Coalition force arrives in a cluster and you can disable several craft with the Havoc's blast.

The Coalition fighters primarily go after the Gamma wing bombers. Order your wingmen to

warning

Protect the Gamma wing bombers at all cost. If both bombers perish, you're sent back to the *Reliant* with a failed mission. As long as one bomber remains intact, you can proceed to the next Nav point and the attack on Latov Base.

target specific Coalition craft. Use any remaining Bandit missiles against the fighters to whittle their numbers down as soon as possible. Stick close to Gamma wing and be sure to engage any fighters specifically targeting the Allied bombers. Once the Coalition fighters have been destroyed or run out of the mission area, the Nanny ship enters to refuel and rearm your fighter. Much like the Coalition convoy, the fighters will jump out of the mission area if it takes you too long to eliminate them. Should any fighters escape to warn Coalition Command, you'll have to face an additional Badanov carrier and five Sabre fighters during the attack on Latov Base.

Cycle through friendly targets to locate the Nanny ship. Use your afterburner to approach, and then enter escort position by flying through the red wire frame. Once inside, the Nanny pulls you in and replenishes your afterburner fuel, missiles, and countermeasures. Activate your jump drive to proceed to Nav point 3 and Latov Base.

Objective: Destroy the Latov Base's communication tower.

Target Latov Base and use your afterburner to approach it. If any Coalition fighters escaped the last Nav point, you'll face a Badanov carrier and five Sabres between the area's starting point and Latov Base. As you approach, a wingman announces that you must destroy Latov's communication tower before the Coalition radios for reinforcements. Order wingmen to engage any fighters in the area while you cycle through subtargets to locate the communication tower (see Figure 6.7). Use primary weapons against the tower; it shouldn't take many shots before the subtarget explodes. Failing to destroy the communication tower in 60 seconds allows the base to alert ten Coalition Saracen fighters. Keeping Gamma wing safe will be nearly impossible when they arrive, so be sure to terminate that tower as soon as you're assigned the objective.

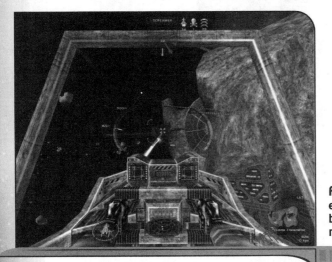

Figure 6.7: Divert power to the engines or use your ship's afterburner to reach Latov's communication tower.

Objective: Destroy the Latov Base's defense turrets.

With the communication tower destroyed, your next objective is to eliminate the Latov Base's laser turrets. Cycle through subtargets to locate the turrets. As you're likely to take hits from the turrets while doing so, switch on your ship's ECM and divert power to the shields. Slow down as you approach each turret and use small bursts of the afterburner to move to the next target. Keep your wingmen busy with orders to engage any remaining Coalition fighters.

Once the turrets are destroyed, Gamma wing moves in against the Latov Base satellite dish. Immediately target the nearest Coalition fighter (if any remain) and engage it. Use your Bandit missiles in defense of Gamma wing, but save your Jackhammer for Latov's vent shaft. If no Coalition fighters remain in the area, order your wingmen against the Kurgens. If Coalition fighters destroy Gamma wing before the satellite dish is destroyed, you're ordered back to the *Reliant* and the mission ends in failure.

Should you lack a Jackhammer missile or simply miss your shot, don't abort the mission. After a minute, a fellow wingman approaches the vent shaft and fires a Jackhammer inside. You'll lose the thrill of blowing apart Latov Base, but the mission still ends successfully.

Objective: Destroy the Latov Base's vent hatch.
Watch the cut-scene of the satellite dish exploding and listen for orders to target Latov Base's vent hatch. Cycle through Latov's subtargets until you locate the hatch. Use primary weapons to easily eliminate the cover. Keep your wingmen occupied with dogfights against any remaining Coalition fighters or Kurgens.

Objective: Launch a Jackhammer down the vent hatch shaft.
Once the vent hatch is opened, ready your Jackhammer missile. Move out from the shaft and locate the red wire frame position just above the shaft. This position marks the best angle from which to take the shot. When the Jackhammer missiles lock onto the shaft, fire and use your afterburner to retreat to a safe distance. If your missile is on-target, Latov Base will explode into chunks of metal and rock (see Figure 6.8 on the following page).

Activate your jump drive to head back to the *Reliant*. Use your communication menu to request permission to land and conclude the mission.

Mission Debriefing

 Success plus Bonus: Latov and carrier destroyed.

Success: Latov destroyed.

Fail: Latov survives.

Fail: Latov dish not destroyed.

Fail: Gamma wing destroyed.

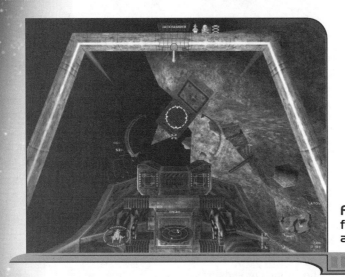

Figure 6.8: Enter the red wire frame for the optimum firing angle.

Mission 11

Mission Date: January 4, 2161

Briefing: Intelligence has received reports that the Coalition has almost finished the construction of a new super carrier, the *Czar*, which, looking at its stats, will outclass any ship in the Alliance fleet. To make matters worse, we've also been informed that the Coalition now has a new advanced Warp Gate system online. If used in conjunction with the *Czar*, the consequences for the Alliance could be dire.

Using captured Coalition data, our tech division has produced a prototype warp projector capable of creating a temporary wormhole big enough for a single fighter to slip through—ideal for covert operations. The warp projector requires 15 seconds to charge before firing; they're still a little unstable, so use them only as directed.

Upon reaching the shipyard facility, your first objective will be to punch a hole through the orbiting satellite defense turrets. Next objective will be to engage any Coalition fighters in the vicinity. With the fighter defense neutralized, move on to the facility's defensive turrets. Once the fighters and defensive turrets are out of the way, Gamma wing will torpedo the *Czar*'s main hull while the target designation ship locates the carrier's twin power cores. With the power core pinpointed, launch your Jackhammer missiles and evacuate the area.

As you've probably assumed by now, this mission is of vital importance; fortunately, you won't be going alone. Coming along for the ride will be a contingent from the Vampires. Due to his experience, squadron leader Klaus Steiner will be in overall command of the mission.

Ship Selection and Missile Load Out

The *Czar*'s laser turrets, the satellite defenses, several Kurgens, and the Loki and Azan fighters necessitate selecting a rugged craft here. Most of the mission's activity takes place in a small area, eliminating the need for a fast ship with an excellent acceleration rating. At the same time, however, you'll likely need an extra fuel pod to offset the lack of afterburner fuel on well-armored ships.

Select either the Grendel or Coyote (if available). The Grendel includes significantly less afterburner fuel, so outfit at least one fuel pod on its missile hardpoints. The Grendel is more durable than the Coyote, but not quite as effective against the Loki and Azan wings that attack. Proceed with the Coyote if you struggled in the protection of the boarding ship in Mission 9. The Mirage or Tempest (if you've released them) also prove effective. Both include ample ECM, and the Tempest features excellent primary weapons and Spectral Shields.

The mission requires two Jackhammer missiles—so don't leave the *Reliant* without them! Save them until the attack on the *Czar*'s inner power core cover. Equip the remaining missile hardpoints with Bandit missiles and one or two fuel pods for extra afterburner resources.

Battle Plan

Objective: Rendezvous with the Vampires.
Launch from the *Reliant* and listen to the message that the Vampires are currently occupied elsewhere; you'll have to begin the mission without them. Watch the cut-scene of Gamma wing launching, then activate the warp projector by pressing the jump-drive key. You'll emerge near Saturn by the shipyard where the *Czar* has docked.

Objective: Warp to the *Czar* and destroy the satellite defenses.
Your first objective is to eliminate the satellite laser turrets that hover around the *Czar*'s perimeter. The shipyard lies a great distance away, so utilize your afterburner to approach the *Czar* and satellites quickly. As you arrive, a wing of Loki fighters and several Kurgens launch from the shipyard to intercept you. Order your wingmen against the Lokis and Kurgens as you concentrate on terminating the satellites (see Figure 6.9).

Cycle through enemy targets until you've located a defense satellite. Don't waste any missiles against them, as it only takes a few primary weapon shots to destroy a satellite. You will be extremely close to the *Czar*'s laser turrets, however, and the Coalition Lokis and Kurgens will also likely target your vessel. Divert power to the shields and switch on your ship's ECM for additional protection. If you selected a craft with Spectral Shields, activate them as well.

> **tip**
>
> You're an easy target while taking out the satellites—especially to Loki fighter missiles. Be on the lookout for notification of an enemy missile lock and be prepared to use countermeasures at a moment's notice.

Continue to eliminate the satellites until a wingman announces that enough are destroyed. Alliance Command sends in the Vampires escorting a marine boarding ship to dock with the *Czar* and extract its shield codes.

Objective: Escort and protect the boarding ship.
Don't stop eliminating satellites once the boarding ship enters—the turrets still pose a threat to it, particularly around the docking point. You can spot this point by the red wire frame adjacent to the *Czar*'s

Figure 6.9: Work your way through the satellites while your wingmen battle the fighter and Kurgen defenses.

hull. Destroy all the satellites that surround this. If the boarding ship is destroyed before completing its two-minute dock with the *Czar*, you're sent back to the *Reliant* and the mission ends in failure.

With a majority of the satellites out of the way, turn your attention to the remaining Loki fighters and the Kurgens. Use your locking missiles against the fighters, but save both Jackhammer missiles for the *Czar*'s power core. During the battle with the Lokis, another Coalition capital ship enters and launches a wing of Azan fighters. Target the nearest one and engage.

The boarding ship will continue to update you on its status via the communication display. If it's taking damage, it will prod you to assist. Eliminate the Loki and Azan fighters as swiftly as possible, then engage the remaining satellites and Kurgens.

When the boarding ship docks, approach its position and check if it's absorbing shots from any Coalition source. If so, locate and quickly destroy the aggressor. The boarding ship docks for two minutes to retrieve the codes. Once finished, it launches off the *Czar*, deciphers the codes, and transmits them to Gamma wing. Watch the cut-scene of Gamma wing destroying the *Czar*'s shield generator. You now have one minute to destroy the ship's power core.

tip

Cycle through friendly targets to locate the boarding ship and its current position. Use your afterburner to quickly intercept it and engage any surrounding Coalition fighters. Any nearby Kurgens will also prove troublesome; order all wingmen against a single Kurgen to eliminate the Coalition corvette quickly.

While the boarding ship is deciphering and transmitting the codes, fly around the back end of the *Czar* and into its rear interior—this is where you'll destroy the power core. Eliminate any laser turrets inside and await attack orders. You'll buy yourself some extra seconds if you're already in position once the order is handed down.

Objective: Destroy the outer power core cover.

With the shield generator down, target the *Czar* and cycle through its subtargets until you locate the service door. You'll need to fly around the rear of the ship and into its interior. Simply follow the target directional indicator after approaching the *Czar*'s back end. Enter the red wire frame near the service door for a premium firing angle. Don't use the Jackhammer missiles against the surface door; blow it apart with primary weapons only.

Objective: Destroy the inner power core cover.

Target the *Czar*'s vent hatch subtarget. You won't be able to use primary weapons to blow through the hatch's durable armor, so wait until one of your Jackhammers locks on and fire. The explosion should blow open the vent hatch and provide access to the power core (see Figure 6.10). While inside the *Czar*, divert power to the shields, switch on your ship's ECM, and activate Spectral Shields if applicable. These extra defenses will help if any of the *Czar*'s laser turrets or remaining satellites have you in their line of sight.

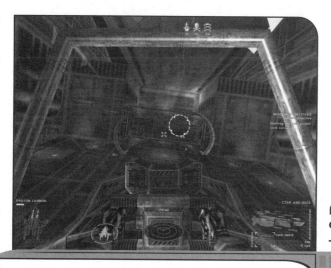

Figure 6.10: The inner power core cover requires a Jackhammer missile.

Objective: Destroy the core with a Jackhammer missile.

With the core exposed, lock on with a Jackhammer missile and launch. Turn your ship around and move full throttle away from the *Czar*. Watch the cut-scene of the *Czar* exploding. Listen for the command to activate your warp projector, then press the jump-drive key to return to the *Reliant* and complete the mission.

Objective: Destroy the *Reliant*'s attackers (If you failed to destroy the Warp Protogate in Mission 3).

Failing to destroy the Warp Gate in the third mission causes an unexpected Coalition fighter and bomber attack upon your arrival at the *Reliant*. Once the attack begins, target the nearest fighter and engage. When the Kamov bombers enter, concentrate on the torpedoes; as soon as you've eliminated a few waves of launched warheads, the Kamovs will jump out of the area. After either the Coalition force jumps out or you destroy them, radio the *Reliant* for permission to land and conclude the mission.

Mission Debriefing

⚡ **Success plus Bonus**: *Czar* destroyed and boarding ship survives.

⚡ **Success**: *Czar* destroyed and boarding ship dead post-docking.

⚡ **Fail**: *Czar* survives.

⚡ **Fail**: Boarding ship dead predocking.

chapter 7

Frontier Operations— Missions 12 to 16

A key victory against the Coalition's new super carrier, the *Czar*, has propelled the Alliance to a series of battle successes. It's not time to celebrate quite yet, though. Colonel McGann, a traitor to the Alliance, is still feeding the Coalition valuable information about ships, weapons, and troop movements.

This chapter includes detailed walkthroughs for the five missions that make up *StarLancer*'s third campaign. The varied campaign begins with numerous dogfights against tough Coalition Basilisks and traitorous Alliance fighters and concludes with harrowing assaults on heavily armed Coalition cruisers. During the campaign you'll confront Colonel McGann and his band of renegade pilots, learn the identity of a second Alliance traitor, assault another Coalition Warp Gate, and take shelter on a new base of operations, the *Yamato*.

Mission 12

Mission Date: March 6, 2161

Briefing: Tech division has informed us that they are about to bring our own Warp Gate system online. However, a lack of fuel cells is holding this up. Fortunately, Intelligence has identified a Coalition mining base that is producing fuel cells for their Warp Gates. Our mission is to liberate some of this fuel and destroy the facility.

You will be providing fighter support for a Japanese squadron called the Ronin, flying off of the *ANS Yamato*. By all accounts they are a top class outfit. Also along for the ride will be a detachment of Rippers; their task will be to grab the fuel cells.

On takeoff, link up with the Rippers and jump ahead to Nav point 1, where you will rendezvous with the Ronin. You must then hold position with the Rippers while the Ronin jump forward on a decoy attack to draw away the base's fighter unit. On their signal, you and the Rippers should move in.

Your first objective will be to take out the base's defensive turrets. Your second objective is to blow the service door to the base's depot hanger. You will then escort the Rippers to the interior of the base. Once inside, the Rippers will locate and secure the fuel cell containers and make a fast exit. You will then tag the remaining fuel cells using your lasers. This will start a fusion buildup, which in turn will create a chain reaction throughout the depot. Get well out of range when it blows. Finally, escort the Rippers to Fort Sherman, and then return to the *Reliant*.

Ship Selection and Missile Load Out

Protecting the Rippers and their fuel cell cargo provides the biggest challenge in this mission. The assault on the Stalag requires a keen sense of timing and direction. While nearly any ship should have success against the Stalag's relatively weak armaments, selecting one with the agility to keep up with Coalition Sabre and Azan fighters is a must. Both the Coyote and Tempest, released upon entering the third campaign, possess enough mobility and firepower to combat the waves of Coalition fighters that threaten the Rippers.

Both feature excellent missile capacity, ECM, and afterburner fuel. The Tempest carries a slight edge in shield strength, primary weaponry, and the Spectral Shields ability, but don't dismiss the Coyote and its mobility advantage and dogfight-friendly Blind Fire. Either fighter should perform well during the mission, though the Coyote's extra agility and Blind Fire will provide the best chance for success against the Coalition attackers.

Anti-fighter warheads should dominate your missile hardpoints, so outfit your craft with Raptor pods or Bandit missiles. The Raptor pod carries three missiles per hardpoint, but individually they don't inflict the damage of a single Bandit warhead.

Battle Plan

Objective: Rendezvous with the Ronin. Launch from the *Reliant* and activate the jump drive when prompted. You'll emerge at the *Yamato* just in time to see the Ronin launch from its hangars. The Ronin immediately jump ahead to attack and divert the fighter contingent guarding the Stalag asteroid base. To cause the diversion, the Ronin retreat slowly after attacking. As soon as you've received the radio message, activate your jump drive to emerge at the Stalag.

Objective: Destroy the external defenses on the Stalag.

Begin your approach to the asteroid base. Don't bother using afterburner fuel to reach the Stalag; you're not pressed for time and you'll need every second of fuel later in the mission. During your approach, the Stalag's front service doors open and five Coalition Lagg and three Coalition Sabre fighters exit and intercept your wing. Target the nearest enemy ship and engage (see Figure 7.1).

Fight the first wave of enemy fighters away from the Stalag base. The asteroid has four laser turrets positioned around the front service door. If you battle the Laggs and Sabres too close to the Stalag, you're just taking extra—and very unnecessary—laser fire that could penetrate your shields and damage your hull.

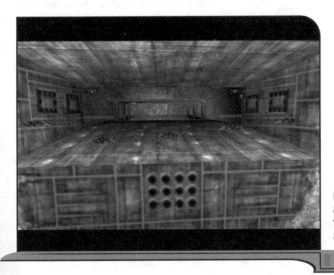

Figure 7.1: Deal with the Lagg and Sabre fighters released from the Stalag before moving against the base's laser turrets.

This first wave of Coalition fighters doesn't pose a threat to the Rippers. Save your secondary weapons to use against the fighters that attack the Ripper ships directly, later on in the mission. Use primary weapons solely to eliminate the Lagg and Sabre fighters. Order your wingmen to engage specific ships to terminate them quickly.

Turn your attention to the Stalag base once the Coalition fighters are destroyed. Four laser turrets are positioned around the vent hatch. Target the Stalag and cycle through its subtargets until you locate the turrets. Switch on your ship's ECM for protection. You should also divert full power to the shields and activate Spectral Shields if available. There are only four turrets placed in a square formation around the vent hatch. Destroy each with your guns.

Objective: Destroy the Stalag's vent hatch.
Cycle through the Stalag's subtargets until you've targeted the vent hatch. Shoot the hatch for a few moments with your primary weapons. Once the hatch explodes open, proceed into the tunnel and to the heart of the Stalag base. Don't bother trying to get inside through the service door—it's impenetrable to your missiles and guns.

Objective: Destroy the internal defenses on the Stalag.
Don't fly directly to the center of the Stalag interior; there are many laser turrets inside and you might not be able to withstand their combined firepower. A wingman tells the 45th that he's going in to investigate, but you can enter through the vent hatch and into the Stalag's interior as well.

Stay inside the entrance tunnel and cycle through the Stalag's subtargets to target the interior laser turrets. Eliminate each turret, one at a time, with primary weapons. Activate your ship's ECM, boost the power to the shields, and use Spectral Shields if available. Destroy as many turrets as possible from the entrance tunnel. Once you've knocked out a number of turrets, proceed inside and eliminate any remaining interior defenses.

warning

If you're inside the Stalag when the base explodes, your ship is destroyed and the funeral cut-scene plays. Have the vent hatch in sight at all times when firing at the fuel cells.

Objective: Protect the Rippers during their pickup.
Destroying the last interior laser turret cues the Rippers to enter the Stalag base through the vent hatch and snag the fuel cells. The Rippers grab the cells one at a time and announce success once they've cleared the vent hatch. There's no threat to the Rippers after you've eliminated the interior laser turrets. Remain inside the Stalag and monitor the Ripper's acquisition of the fuel cells. The first threat arrives after the second Ripper has exited the vent hatch.

Objective: Destroy the fuel cells.
While the Rippers are grabbing the fuel cells, you should get in position to destroy the fuel cells and quickly exit the Stalag through the vent hatch. Hover over the fuel cells and face the vent hatch. As soon as the second Ripper exits the base, begin firing primary weapons at the fuel cells.

After you've destroyed two or three fuel cells, a wingman announces that the chain reaction has begun. Immediately turn to face the vent hatch and use your afterburner to exit the Stalag interior (see Figure 7.2). Ignore the explosions around you and continue through the vent hatch tunnel.

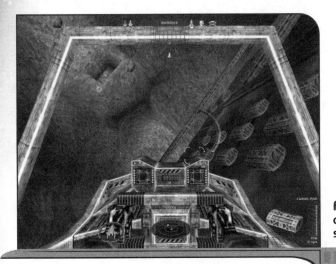

Figure 7.2: Face both the fuel cells and the exit hatch before starting the chain reaction.

Objective: Escort the Rippers back to Fort Carter.

During your escape from the Stalag, six Coalition Azan fighters enter and target the Ripper ships. Order your wingmen to engage the Azan fighters. Do the same yourself as soon as you're clear of the Stalag. Use locking missiles against the Azan. Also, cycle through friendly targets to locate the Ripper ships. Then intercept their positions and attack any Azan fighter attempting to destroy the fuel cells.

Save some locking missiles for one last objective. Once you've eliminated the six Azan ships, you're ordered to jump to Fort Carter and protect the Rippers as they unload the cargo. Upon your arrival, another wing of Azan fighters, plus an ace named Red Dragon, jumps in and attacks the Rippers. Target the nearest Azan and use a Havoc missile to disrupt their electronic systems and buy extra time in defense of the Rippers. If only one Ripper ship survives, the mission is flagged as a partial failure. You must save both Rippers in order to complete the mission successfully.

While the Azans are temporarily disabled, order your wingmen to take on specific enemy fighters. Use any remaining locking missiles on nearby Azans. Keep tabs on the Rippers location and intercept any enemy fighter attacking the fuel cells.

Once you've neutralized the Azan threat, the Rippers safely dock with Fort Carter. Activate the jump drive when prompted to return to the *Reliant* and end the mission.

Mission Debriefing

 Success plus Bonus: Two Rippers survive, and Stalag and Red Dragon destroyed.

 Success: Two Rippers survive and Stalag destroyed.

 Partial Success: Two Rippers survive and Stalag not destroyed.

 Partial Fail: One Ripper survives.

 Fail: Both Rippers destroyed.

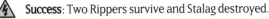

Mission 13

Mission Date: April 15, 2161

Briefing: Our supply lines to the front have recently come under attack from some old friends of yours, Colonel McGann and company. High Command wants them out of the way and we've been given the gig—we won't disappoint.

We have got a large shipment of arms on its way to the front and we've made sure that word has leaked out about it. With any luck McGann and friends will turn up expecting some easy pickings. The convoy's fighter escort is under instructions to fire off a few rounds and then bug out.

Your orders are to track McGann and the shipment back to their base; then and only then will you be given the green light to strike. Wipe out McGann's fighters and Gamma wing will do the rest.

Ship Selection and Missile Load Out

The mission to smoke out Colonel McGann features several difficult fighter engagements and a single attack on a lightly-armed base. Although the base does carry the deadly Ion Cannon, no amount of armor or shielding will save your ship should you be struck. For this mission, the best dogfighting ship available should be selected and armed with plenty of anti-fighter warheads.

The Coyote's powerful mix of speed, agility, missile capacity, and Blind Fire makes it a difficult choice to pass up. Another possibility is the Mirage. It features better mobility and primary weapons than the Coyote, but lacks missile carrying capacity and Blind Fire. If you rely more on primary weapons to defeat enemy craft, select the Mirage and its powerful guns. Should you desire more missiles and hope the Blind Fire ability offsets weaker primary weapons, then select the Coyote.

Equip your ship with Raptor pods or Bandit missiles. You should also select one or two Havoc missiles to temporarily disable key enemy fighters. Use the Havocs at Nav point 2 against the Saracen attack or save them for later use against McGann and Viper. Imp missiles, which don't disable ships but instead knock out their shields, are also effective against McGann and Viper. Follow up the Imp with a volley of Raptors for optimum damage.

Battle Plan

Objective: Shadow the convoy.

The *Crimson Sky* jumps in along with Colonel Tanner and the Pumas. Tanner and the Pumas will jump ahead along with the *Crimson Sky* and the convoy; they'll stay one Nav point ahead of you in order to bait McGann into capturing the homing device-equipped *Crimson Sky*. Moments after the convoy jumps to Nav point 1, a wingman orders the 45th and Gamma wing to follow.

Objective: Protect Gamma wing from the Coalition fighter wing.

You'll meet up with the *Crimson Sky* and the Pumas briefly at Nav point 1. Once you're in, though, Colonel Tanner orders the convoy and Pumas to proceed to Nav point 2. As you await orders to continue on, a wing of Coalition Saracen and Sabre fighters enters and targets Gamma wing.

Target and intercept the nearest Saracen or Sabre. You should also cycle through friendly targets to keep tabs on Gamma wing's position. At least one of the two Gamma wing bombers must survive in order to complete the mission; if both are destroyed in the fighter attack, the mission is aborted and you jump back to the *Reliant* in failure (see Figure 7.3).

Figure 7.3: Protect Gamma wing from the Saracen attack or the mission will be aborted.

Have a Havoc missile ready for the enemy fighters. As soon as the enemy fighters enter, target the nearest Coalition vessel and use your afterburner to intercept it. When the Havoc missile locks, fire it at the lead craft. The resulting explosion should disable most, if not all, of the fighter group. Finish them off, but remember to conserve as many locking missiles as possible.

Objective: Destroy the rogue wing. After the Saracen fighters are destroyed, the convoy announces that it's under attack at Nav point 2. The shuttle containing the crew of the *Crimson Sky* jumps back to Nav 1—with four renegade fighters in tow. These members of McGann's traitorous group spot the 45th and Gamma wing immediately. Allied Command announces that you have two minutes to eliminate the renegade wing before they alert McGann of the Alliance's plan.

> **warning**
>
> If there are still renegade ships left at Nav point 1 two minutes after the battle began, McGann learns of the Alliance plan. The mission is aborted and you're ordered back to the *Reliant*.

The renegade ships aren't especially tough, so try to hold on to as many Bandit or Raptor missiles as possible for the more difficult fight at the end of this mission. Target the nearest renegade ship (remember that the ex-Alliance ship will appear green on your targeting display) and engage. Order your wingmen to gang up against one renegade ship to hasten the destruction of the rebels. Battle all four ships to wipe out the wing and keep the Alliance plan from McGann's ears.

The Pumas return to Nav point 1 once the renegade pilots are destroyed. Tanner announces that the tracking device is working perfectly. The wings are ordered to proceed back to Nav 2 once McGann and his fellow pilots have fled from the *Crimson Sky*'s destruction. Jump to Nav point 2 when prompted.

At Nav 2 you'll spot the *Crimson Sky*, crippled and spinning with cargo pods extracted. Colonel Tanner announces they have a trace on McGann's position. After some additional pilot chatter, you're ordered to initiate the warp projector and enter McGann's territory along with the Pumas and Gamma wing.

Objective: Destroy the rogue base defense cannon.

Ahead you'll spot Fort Vanguard, an abandoned Alliance base that McGann is apparently using as a base of operations. There are no enemy fighters in the area, so Gamma wing is ordered to hold back while the 45th and Pumas investigate the abandoned station.

Approach the base slowly without wasting afterburner fuel. A few moments after you arrive alongside Fort Vanguard, a turret positioned at the bottom of the base initializes and destroys one of your wingmen with a single burst. New orders are sent to destroy the turret, referred to as the Ion Cannon.

The Ion Cannon isn't especially durable, but if you stick around it too long, the turret will track you with its red laser beam and then destroy you in a single shot. If you equipped a Jackhammer missile, use it against the cannon for easy damage and then finish off the turret with primary weapons. If the red beam tracks you, use your afterburner to reach the top of the base and climb out of the Ion Cannon's line of fire. Return to the turret when clear and finish the job. Ignore the less threatening Loki fighters while you destroy the turret.

> **tip**
>
> You can actually destroy the cannon before you know of its existence. Just fly up under the base and locate the large turret attached to its bottom. Then use primary weapons to destroy it. Coalition Lokis will immediately jump in and attack, but you won't have to worry about getting shredded by the Ion Cannon.

Objective: Take out McGann.

Concentrate on the Loki fighters once the Ion Cannon has been destroyed. When the last Loki is eliminated, McGann enters along with several renegade and Coalition fighters. Success in the mission requires the destruction of McGann and his fighter. Cycle through enemy targets until you've selected his craft. Quickly intercept and fire several Bandit missiles when locked onto McGann's ship (see Figure 7.4).

If McGann escapes, the mission's entire plan is for naught. You're ordered back to the *Reliant* and the mission ends in failure. Therefore, don't

> **tip**
>
> A shield-destroying Imp missile, followed by one or two Raptor missiles, is a deadly combination. Use the tactic on Colonel McGann's ship for a quick kill.

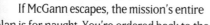

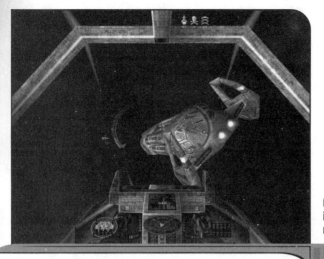

Figure 7.4: Target McGann immediately and use your remaining locking missiles.

battle other renegade or Coalition ships before proceeding against McGann. Target his fighter immediately and use every means necessary to destroy him.

After dealing with McGann, complete the mission objectives by cycling to the next renegade or Coalition target. Continue to destroy each fighter until the area is secure. Some of the renegade pilots, especially those in nimble ships like the Naginata, prove elusive targets. The Coyote's Blind Fire ability will be especially useful here. Use primary weapons against McGann's wingmen and save a few Bandit missiles for the next objective.

Objective: Take out Viper.

Your old friend and fellow 45th pilot Viper jumps in after McGann's wing has been destroyed; apparently Viper wasn't killed in the jump drive accident after all. Target Viper first and engage. Use any remaining Bandit missiles against his craft. Cycle through the other renegade and Coalition targets once you've eliminated Viper's ship. If Viper escapes, you still complete the original mission (dealing with McGann) successfully. Terminating the traitorous Viper completes this mission's bonus objective.

With Viper either dead or escaped, Gamma wing moves in to launch torpedoes against Fort Vanguard. As they approach, finish off any remaining fighters or laser turrets. Once the base explodes, Alliance Command orders the Pumas and the 45th back to the *Reliant*, concluding the mission.

Mission Debriefing

 Success plus Bonus: McGann and Viper killed, rogue base destroyed.

Success: McGann killed, rogue base destroyed.

 Fail plus Kick out: Gamma wing destroyed at Nav I.

Fail plus Kick out: Four renegades not destroyed within two minutes at Nav I.

 Fail plus Kick out: McGann escapes.

Mission 14

Mission Date: May 25, 2161
Briefing: Our spies have located the nerve center of Coalition Warp Gate operations. The facility controls gate operations throughout this sector, along with holding much of the Coalition's fuel for Warp Gates across the system. The advanced Warp Gate located here serves as a hub for much ship movement. Loss of this base would severely hinder their ability to quickly move ships around.

The Tigers and Gamma wings will warp to a designated point close to the facility. The Tigers' first objective is to eliminate any sentry turrets and enemy fighters they may find on the outer perimeter. Reports are sketchy, but you will probably also encounter some heavier ships near the base. As always, we will keep you updated with objectives, as the picture becomes clearer.

Once the defenses have been smashed, Gamma wing will start their run and launch torpedoes on the facility and then rendezvous back with the *Reliant*. The Tigers will finish the job by taking out the advanced Warp Gate. Its four power cores must all be wrecked to ensure complete destruction.

Ship Selection and Missile Load Out

The attack on the Coalition research base and Warp Gate requires durability and firepower. This mission also calls for combat against heavily armed Kurgens and a few fighter skirmishes. Endurance should be favored over agility; the dogfighting in the mission is light and the ability to survive close encounters with the base and Warp Gate's laser turrets takes precedence.

Both the Crusader and Tempest carry enough shield strength and armor to be effective. Furthermore, both possess the key Spectral Shields ability that will likely save your hide during the attack on the base or Warp Gate. The Tempest's extra missile capacity and nearly double ECM capability make it the better choice of the two.

Equip a few Raptor pods or Bandit missiles for use against the fighters. Screamer pods should assist in knocking out the immobile Warp Gate power cells, but if you're selecting the Crusader or Tempest, you should have plenty of primary weapon firepower to do the job.

Battle Plan

Objective: Escort Gamma wing to the drop off point.
The Reliant launches both the 45th and Gamma wing. According to orders, the squadrons warp ahead to the next Nav point. Gamma wing will be left there while the 45th proceeds one more Nav point to the Coalition Warp Gate to eliminate fighter cover, satellite defenses, and laser turrets. When prompted, activate your jump drive to open the warp projector.

Objective: Jump to the Coalition Warp Gate.

Arrive at Nav point 1 to drop off Gamma wing. Listen to your wingmen discuss the situation at the upcoming Coalition Warp Gate. Hit your jump drive when prompted to proceed to Nav point 2 and the Warp Gate.

Objective: Destroy the research base defenses.

You're not on a time table upon the arrival at the Coalition Warp Gate, so take the time to eliminate all fighter cover in the area before proceeding against the research base's laser turrets. Several Kurgens defending the area should be eliminated to safeguard the arrival of Gamma wing. Once the Coalition fighters are destroyed, order your wingmen against the Kurgens. Assist them and remove the Coalition corvettes quickly. With fighter cover eradicated, target the research base and cycle through subtargets to select its laser turrets (see Figure 7.5).

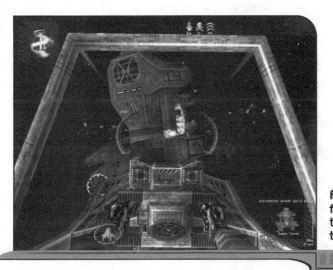

Figure 7.5: Eliminate the fighter cover before assaulting the research base and its turrets.

The research base's defenses and the Kurgens produce a substantial amount of laser fire. Switch on your ship's ECM and divert power to the shields when battling fighters around the base and Kurgens. If you selected a ship with Spectral Shields, activate them once you're in range of either the base or a Kurgen for further protection.

While you're working on the research base's laser turrets, keep the wingmen occupied with the Kurgens. Minimize damage as much as possible by using your ECM or Spectral Shields when close to the base's laser turrets. You should also divert full power to the shields since you won't need your engines or a fast gun recharge against the immobile and poorly armored targets. Don't forget to equalize power once Gamma wing enters the area.

Objective: Protect Gamma wing during its torpedo run.

The destruction of the research base's satellite and laser turret defenses cues the arrival of Gamma wing. Cycle through enemy targets to locate any remaining Coalition defenses or fighters. Immediately attack anything that still remains in the area.

If you've secured the area for Gamma wing, move toward the Coalition Warp Gate in preparation for your attack. As soon as Gamma wing destroys the research base with torpedoes, you'll be ordered to obliterate the Warp Gate's four power cells.

Objective: Destroy the power cells on the Warp Gate.

After Gamma wing destroys the research base, target the Coalition Warp Gate and cycle through sub-targets until you locate the nearest power cell. The cells won't offer much resistance against primary weapons (see Figure 7.6). If you have any locking missiles or Screamer pods remaining, you can use them against the power cells (the cells are the last objective in the mission).

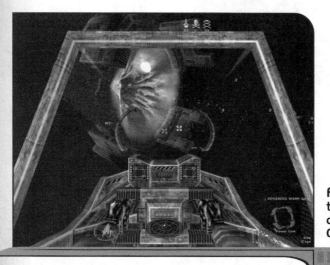

Figure 7.6: Work quickly through the Warp Gate's power cells to avoid the arrival of the Coalition carrier.

Attack the power cells by reducing your speed to a minimum; this should enable you to line up your crosshairs much more easily. When you've eliminated one power cell, use short bursts of your ship's after-burner to reach the others. During your assault on the remaining cells, a Coalition carrier, the *Krasny*, will begin to enter through the gate. If you're quick enough in disposing of the remaining cells, the resulting Warp Gate explosion will destroy the *Krasny* and complete the mission's bonus objective.

If the *Krasny* makes it through the Warp Gate, Allied Command orders the 45th to return to the *Reliant*, even if Warp Gate power cells

warning

Failure to destroy the Coalition's advanced Warp Gate introduces additional fighter attacks in subsequent missions. If you want to make life easier for yourself, eliminate the Warp Gate before you leave the area.

remain intact. Should you retreat without destroying the Warp Gate, you won't achieve full success in the mission. The *Krasny* doesn't significantly impede your attack on the power cells, so ignore the order to jump out and finish the job. When all the cells have been destroyed, activate your jump drive to return to the *Reliant*.

Mission Debriefing

 Success plus Bonus: Research base, Coalition Warp Gate, and *Krasny* destroyed.

Success: Research base and Coalition Warp Gate destroyed.

Partial Success: Research base destroyed.

Mission 15

Mission Date: June 24, 2161
Briefing: Our long-range scanners have been picking up traces of Coalition ion trails in this sector for over two days now. Captain Foster wants a general sweep of these four Nav points, so see what you can dig up. If you come across anything, report back to the *Reliant* and we will take it from there.

Ship Selection and Missile Load Out

In one of the most diverse missions thus far, Mission 15 finds you battling agile, and often cloaked, Coalition Basilisk fighters; intercepting Kamovs and their torpedoes; and making an assault on two well-armed Coalition cruisers. Protecting the Alliance convoy from fighters and bombers determines mission success, so consider selecting an agile dogfighting ship over a tougher one.

The Coyote and Tempest work best, because of their excellent mobility, decent durability, and ample missile hardpoints. Select the Coyote if you favor the Blind Fire ability and its effectiveness in dogfighting. Pilot the Tempest should you desire Spectral Shields, useful both in fighter combat and against the two cruisers at the mission's end.

Outfit your ship's missile hardpoints with a mixture of Raptor and Bandit missiles. Also take along several Vagabond missiles for use against the cloaking Basilisks you'll engage at the first Nav point.

Battle Plan

Objective: Survey the area for Coalition hunting packs.
Enriquez and Captain Foster order you to sweep specific Nav points for Coalition activity. Launch from the *Reliant* and listen to the pilot communication. Activate your jump drive when you're given the order to proceed to the next Nav point.

Objective: Destroy all enemies in the immediate area.

At Nav 1, a wingman detects unusual energy levels moments before nine Coalition Basilisk fighters enter. The Basilisks attack from all sides in groups of three. There's no time limit to destroy them, so be patient and don't waste too many secondary weapons. Because they cloak periodically, it could take several minutes to eliminate the entire force. Target and engage the nearest fighter. Try to keep the Basilisk in your crosshairs as long as possible while you use primary weapons and ready secondary weapons (see Figure 7.7).

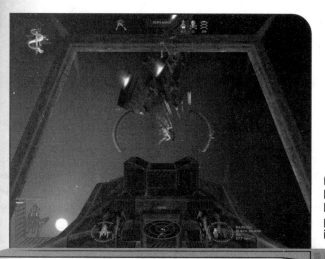

Figure 7.7: The cloaking Basilisks provide quite a challenge. Outfit your ship with plenty of locking missiles, including Vagabonds.

A wing of Coalition Sabre fighters enters once the Basilisks have been eliminated. Once again, you aren't pressured by time constraints to finish off the Sabres. The lighter Coalition fighters aren't as agile as the Basilisks and don't pose the problems that the cloaking ships offer. Preserve your locking missiles for later in the mission; terminate the Sabres with primary weapons only.

The Sabres will eventually jump out if they're not destroyed. Once you've eliminated the Coalition wing or the Sabres have jumped out, Captain Foster radios the 45th from the bridge of the *Reliant*. Apparently a Coalition carrier group is closing in on the defenseless *Reliant*. He orders the 45th to rendezvous with the *Victorious*. When prompted, activate your ship's jump drive to proceed to the next Nav point.

> **tip**
>
> Equipping Vagabond missiles on your ship's hardpoints will prove effective against the Basilisk wings. Although the Vagabond doesn't cause as much damage as the Bandit locking missiles, the Vagabond can maintain a lock even if the Basilisk pilot activates the cloaking device.

Objective: Protect the convoy from possible attack.

You'll arrive at the *Victorious*, a large Alliance capital ship flying alongside an Allied convoy. Enriquez enters soon after you arrive. Listen to the radio communication and prepare your remaining Vagabond and Bandit missiles for battle.

A group of Coalition Basilisk fighters are first on the scene. Order your wingmen against them and target the nearest Basilisk yourself. Be prepared to alter your course to defend the *Victorious* and convoy against torpedo attack at any time, however. As soon as Allied Command announces the presence of Coalition Kamov torpedo bombers and launched warheads, target them by using the target-nearest-torpedo key and use your afterburner to intercept.

Don't hesitate to use the rest of your locking missiles against the torpedoes. The remaining fighters in the mission aren't especially tough and saving the Alliance convoy from destruction determines the mission's success or failure.

> **tip**
>
> You can still achieve full success and bonuses on the mission if the Kamov torpedoes only destroy three of the convoy vessels.

Objective: Take out the torpedoes and then destroy any fighters.

The torpedo barrage launched by the Coalition Kamov is the most difficult to face in the game thus far, as each bomber releases its entire payload at the Alliance convoy. Don't let the number of locked torpedoes overwhelm you (see Figure 7.8). Target the nearest one and use your afterburner to approach it. As you get close, match its speed so you avoid colliding with the warhead. Destroy the torpedo with guns or missiles and then cycle to the next one.

Divert full power to the engines if you're running low on afterburner fuel. Most of the torpedoes are fired from the same vicinity, so you shouldn't have to travel long to locate another warhead.

Figure 7.8: The Kamovs launch a fierce volley of torpedoes.

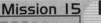

If a Kamov bomber remains in the area after you've eliminated all active warheads, destroy it with primary weapons.

Once all Coalition attackers have been eliminated, Captain Foster radios from the bridge of the *Reliant* with horrible news. His battle against a Coalition carrier has gone poorly, leaving the *Reliant* heavily damaged and still under attack. Watch the cut-scene of Foster's last stand. In a valiant move, Captain Foster manages to repel a final assault on the Coalition carrier. He then maneuvers the *Reliant* to ramming speed and smashes into the hull of the enemy carrier. When the cut-scene completes, listen to Enriquez and your wingmen commenting on the situation. Once you're prompted, activate your jump drive to proceed to the next mission area.

A second wave of fighters and Kamov bombers enters once the cut scene has finished. Order your wingmen to take on the Coalition Azan fighters while you defend the convoy from the torpedoes.

Objective: Take out the *Kiev's* shield generator.

Here you'll find the *Yamato* engaged with two Coalition cruisers. Allied Command orders you against the first of these, the *Kiev*, in an attack run to destroy its shield generator. Coalition Saracen fighters also occupy the area. Order your wingmen to engage them, but you should stay out of this scrap.

Cycle through targets until you've selected the *Kiev*, then use the subtarget key to locate the shield generator. Approach the vessel and use your primary weapons, or any remaining missiles, to knock out the shield generator. With its shields down, the *Kiev* is a sitting duck for the torpedoes launched from the *Yamato*.

tip

Save some afterburner fuel for your attack run against the *Yevstafiy*, which lies a decent distance away from the destroyed *Kiev*. If you don't reach the *Yevstafiy* and destroy its shield generator quickly, the Coalition cruiser will jump out of the mission area and you'll lose the bonus objective.

Objective: Take out the *Yevstafiy's* shield generator.

After the cut-scene of the *Yamato* destroying the *Kiev*, Allied Command orders you on a similar attack run against the *Yevstafiy's* shield generator. Repeat the tactics used to take out the *Kiev* and you'll soon see the *Yamato* destroy the *Yevstafiy* (see Figure 7.9).

Objective: Protect the *Yamato* from any hostile fire.

With the two Coalition cruisers out of the picture, cycle through any remaining enemy targets and engage them. You'll likely face a few leftover Saracen fighters. The mission concludes once all Coalition forces have either fled or have been destroyed. Open up the communication display and request permission to land on your new base of operations, the *ANS Yamato*.

Figure 7.9: The *Yevstafiy* doesn't hang around long once the *Kiev's* shield generator is down. Annihilate the *Yevstafiy's* shield generator quickly.

Mission Debriefing

 Success plus Bonus: Zero to three convoy ships destroyed; *Kiev* and *Yevstafiy* destroyed.

Success: Zero to three convoy ships destroyed; *Kiev* or *Yevstafiy* survive.

Partial Success: Four to six convoy ships destroyed; *Kiev* and *Yvestafiy* destroyed.

Partial Fail: Four to six convoy ships destroyed; *Kiev* or *Yvestafiy* survive.

Fail: Seven to nine convoy ships destroyed.

Mission 16

Mission Date: July 11, 2161
Briefing: The sad loss of Captain Foster has been felt across the Alliance, but we will make sure his sacrifice was not in vain. For the first time in this war, we are beginning to turn things around—and the Coalition knows it! To capitalize on this, we intend to begin counterattacks immediately.

The *ANS Yamato*, with the Ronin and Tigers, will engage the *CS Morzov*, while the Alliance carrier *ANS Bremen* and the Vampire squadron take on the *CS Pukov*, base ship of the infamous Black Guard.

Tackle the *Morzov's* fighters first, then go to work on her flak turrets. Gamma wing will be waiting to move in as soon as they get the green light. Our two targets are currently within striking distance of each other, so be prepared to offer support if the other group gets into trouble.

Ship Selection and Missile Load Out

Much like the previous mission, Mission 16 features a difficult fight against a large wing of Basilisk fighters as well as an assault on a well-armed and heavily-armored cruiser, the *Morzov*.

Select a ship based on your success in the previous mission. If you excel at dogfighting, but need extra armament and protection for a capital ship assault, then choose the Tempest. With its Spectral Shields and powerful primary weapons, the Tempest performs better against the *Morzov* and still possesses the agility to keep up with the Basilisk fighters.

Pick the Coyote if you're more adept at capital ship assaults and tend to struggle against agile fighters. The Coyote's Blind Fire provides an edge over the Tempest when fighting in close quarters. Overall, though, the Tempest's mix of mobility, durability, and firepower make it the best selection.

Equip Bandit missiles and Raptor pods on the majority of your ship's hardpoints. Take some Vagabond missiles for use against the Basilisk fighters and either a Screamer pod or a Jackhammer to blast apart the *Morzov*'s engines.

Battle Plan

Objective: Initiate attack on the *Sharov* transport and *Morzov*.
Launch from the *Yamato* and await orders. As Enriquez reiterates the plan against the *Sharov* transport, a Warp Gate opens and Coalition fighters and Kamov torpedo bombers enter to assault the *Yamato*. Despite the attack, Enriquez orders you to jump to the *Sharov*'s position. Activate your jump drive when prompted.

As you enter, the *Sharov* transport inexplicably jumps out, leaving the *Morzov* alone—but only for a moment! A wing of Basilisk fighters, including the Black Guard ace Nicolai Petrov, and two Kurgen corvettes jump in (see Figure 7.10). Moments later, eight Sabre fighters emerge from the *Morzov*'s hangar. Be prepared for a series of tough dogfights!

Objective: Engage Nicolai Petrov and fighter support.
The Black Guard Basilisk fighters provide a difficult dogfight because of their extreme agility and intermittent cloaking devices. Order your wingmen to engage specific ships and target the closest fighter yourself. The Alliance's Blind Fire ability (equipped on the Coyote and Predator) helps keep your primary weapons affixed on the mobile Basilisk.

The Sabres are much easier, and quickly destroyed, targets at this point in the mission. If you're taking too much damage from multiple enemy fighters, concentrate your targeting on the Sabres. Eliminate them quickly and then return your attention to the Black Guard.

While they don't carry the damage potential of some of the Bandits, Vagabond missiles will

warning

As the *Morzov*'s laser turrets are extremely powerful, selecting a ship with Spectral Shields will certainly assist in assaulting it. If you don't, be sure to activate your ECM when around the *Morzov* and divert full power to your ship's shields.

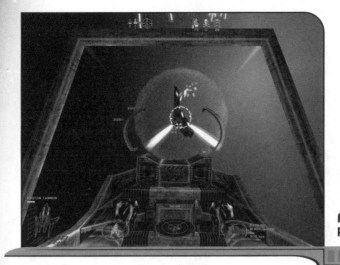

Figure 7.10: Destroy Nicolai Petrov and his Basilisk wing.

maintain a lock even if a Basilisk engages its cloak. Don't use all your locking missiles against Petrov and his gang; you'll face additional Basilisk fighters and another Coalition ace at the end of the mission.

Once all the Basilisk and Sabre fighters are eliminated, you're ordered against the two Kurgens. Open the communication menu and order your wingmen against one Kurgen while you engage the other. Switch on your ECM and divert full power to the shields, particularly if you've suffered hull damage.

Objective: Destroy the *Morzov's* shield generator.

With fighter and Kurgen cover destroyed, it's time to move against the *Morzov*. Target it and cycle through its subtargets until you locate the shield generator. Approach the *Morzov* and locate the highlighted section. Destroy the shield generator with primary weapons. You'll find the generator a bit more durable than those you've run across in previous missions. You may have to perform several rapid attack runs to avoid hovering within range of the *Morzov's* laser turrets.

Objective: Destroy the *Morzov's* engines.

Once the shield generator has been destroyed, quickly cycle through the *Morzov's* subtargets until you locate its engines. Twelve Coalition Lagg fighters enter between the destruction of the *Morzov's* shield generator and your attack on its engines. Ignore the Lagg fighters; you don't have much time to disable the *Morzov's* engine systems (see Figure 7.11).

Approach the engine closely and use primary and secondary weapons. The *Morzov* carries two separate engines. As soon as you've

warning

You must take down the *Morzov's* shield generator before attempting to destroy its engines. Your weapons can't penetrate the shield protecting the *Morzov's* twin engines.

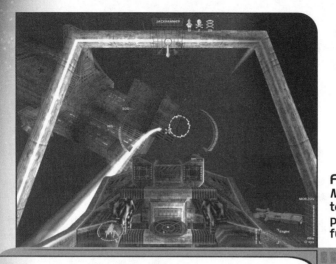

Figure 7.11: Blast the *Morzov*'s engines with missiles to disable the cruiser as fast as possible. Jackhammers are useful here.

destroyed the first, make sure you're targeting the other (or know its precise location) and use primary and secondary weapons to eliminate the engine system. Combining a single Jackhammer, or a volley of Screamer missiles, with your guns works well.

This mission's success depends solely on the destruction of the *Morzov*. If it jumps before the *Yamato* fires its torpedoes, the mission is flagged as a failure. Once the *Yamato* enters, it fires torpedoes at the *Morzov*'s exposed hull—as long as you've disabled its engines. If not, the *Morzov* jumps and escapes destruction.

Objective: Jump out and assist the Vampires.

After the *Morzov* is either destroyed or has escaped, the *Bremen* and Vampires radio a distress call. Although Coalition wings of Lagg, Sabre, and Kamov ships enter, Enriquez orders you to jump to the *Bremen*'s position and rendezvous with the Vampires.

The *Bremen* has already been destroyed as you enter; a brief cut-scene depicts its tumbling wreck of metal. The 45th opens communication with a lone escape pod occupied by a Vampire pilot. But, after a brief conversation, Ivan Petrov

tip

If there is no remaining fighter cover in the area, the *Morzov* jumps out very quickly after you've eliminated its shield generator. To prevent this, work on the *Morzov*'s shield generator and engines at the start of the mission instead of engaging Petrov's Black Guard.

tip

Save some locking missiles, either Raptor or Bandit, for use against Ivan Petrov. Fire your remaining missiles into his Basilisk fighter to cause quick damage. Continue to pound on his ship with primary weapons until he orders a retreat.

(brother of ex-Coalition Ace Nicolai Petrov), enters in a cloaked Basilisk fighter and annihilates the defenseless pod.

Objective: Engage Ivan Petrov and fighter support.

Ivan Petrov attacks with a wing of Black Guard Basilisk fighters. Trying to take on so many Basilisk fighters is a daunting task. Instead, go immediately after Ivan himself. Once you've sufficiently damaged his ship or destroyed part of his wing, he orders the Black Guard wing to retreat from the mission area.

With the area secure, Enriquez orders you to land on the *Yamato* to complete the mission.

Mission Debriefing

⚠ **Success**: *Morzov* destroyed.

⚠ **Fail**: *Morzov* survives.

chapter 8

The Advance to Titan— Missions 17 and 18

After impressive victories against Alliance traitors Colonel McGann and the ex-45th Volunteer, Viper, and an advanced Warp Gate, Allied Command orchestrates a daring operation to capture a Coalition Admiral. While the plan may be sound, its consequences could have lasting effects on the Alliance.

This chapter features walkthroughs for the two missions that comprise *StarLancer's*'s fourth campaign. Consisting of the kidnapping of a Coalition Admiral and an assault on an Ion Cannon platform, these missions hold great importance for the future of the Alliance. Thankfully, Allied Command offers the Tigers three new advanced fighters, all possessing superior weaponry and statistics over the vessels previously available.

Mission 17

Mission Date: August 11, 2161

Briefing: We are starting our push to liberate Titan; if we succeed, we will have secured a major resource and production center which will help support our fleet's needs.

We have an advantage. Our Intelligence people have finally broken the captured ConNexus code, giving us access to planned Coalition movements. These include the imminent arrival of a high-ranking Admiral to the Coalition frontline. This is an opportunity we can't turn down, especially after the loss of the Vampires and Captain Foster.

We are currently tracking the Admiral's flotilla; it consists of escort fighters, gunboats, and a Berijev Command ship, most likely containing the Admiral. The Ronin and Tiger squadrons will be deployed to intercept and engage this group. We need the Admiral alive for a number of reasons; do not under any circumstances destroy the Command ship.

Ship Selection and Missile Load Out

Speed takes precedence over strength in a mission that requires split-second timing. An early attack against agile Coalition Sabre fighters demands speed and firepower; if you don't eliminate the Sabres within one minute, the pilots warn the Berijev Command ship of your arrival. Saving an escape pod later in the mission demands equal portions of speed and mobility.

Command offers three new Alliance fighters for this mission—though you may have had access to them previously if your kill score was great enough. Each new arrival possesses amazing ability, so make your ship selection from one of the three.

Of the new craft, the Patriot features the best mix of sheer speed, agility, and acceleration—although at the expense of armor and missile hardpoints. Powerful primary weapons and the Blind Fire ability make the Patriot the best fighter for the mission. The Reaper also offers Blind Fire ability, but carries additional missile hardpoints and better armor at the expense of speed. The Wolverine is the least agile of the three ships, but more than makes up for its cumbersomeness with abundant ECM, afterburner fuel, mission hardpoints, and the unique Reverse Thrust ability.

Consider the Patriot for its speed advantage over the other two Alliance ships. If you're one to use the afterburner as your primary source of acceleration, consider the Wolverine and its speed-friendly fuel capacity. This vessel should perform admirably, especially if you're concerned about armor class and ECM around the laser turrets of Kurgens and the Berijev.

Outfit the majority of your ship's hardpoints with the now available Hawk pods; you'll receive four satisfactory missiles with each pod. The Hawk is a fast locking missile that doesn't quite do the damage of the Raptor or Bandit, but you can carry many more of them. Consider a Havoc for the Sabres at the first Nav point and a Screamer pod or two for the Berijev's subsystems.

Battle Plan

Objective: Jump out to enemy scouting territory and eliminate any Coalition fighters. Launch from the *Yamato* and listen to the orders from Allied Command and your fellow wingmen. When prompted, activate your ship's jump drive to proceed to the first Nav point.

As you enter, you'll encounter a Coalition Sabre fighter patrol. Listen to a fellow wingman over the communication system. He warns that the Alliance can only jam the Sabres' communication signal for 60 seconds. If the Sabres aren't dispatched within that time, they'll relay a message back to the Coalition to warn of the impending attack (see Figure 8.1).

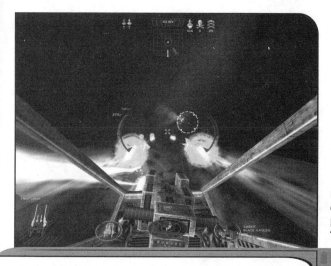

Figure 8.1: Use missiles to destroy the Coalition Sabres—prevent that communication from getting through!

You likely won't have time to order your wingmen to engage specific fighters, so work quickly and immediately target the nearest Sabre yourself. Don't be stingy with (but also don't overuse) your Hawk missiles—quickly knocking out the small wing of Sabres saves you aggravation later on in the mission. Though it helps to eliminate the Sabres within the 60 second time limit, don't attempt the effort at all costs. Remember that you'll still need Hawk missiles and afterburner fuel late in the mission. You're ordered to the next Nav point once the Sabres are either destroyed or jump out. Activate your jump drive when ordered.

Objective: Destroy both Kurgens.

You'll emerge at the next mission area containing the Berijev Command ship, two Kurgens, and a large wing of Coalition Kossac fighters. Ronin orders your wing against the Kurgen corvettes while it handles the Kossac fighters. Cycle through enemy targets until you've located a Kurgen, then order all of Alpha wing against that ship while you assault the other.

While not extremely dangerous, the Kurgen does carry a medium-sized arsenal of laser turrets. As you approach, switch on your ship's ECM and divert additional power to the shields if you've already taken hull damage. Save your secondary weapons for use against the fighters you'll encounter later in the mission and destroy the Kurgen with primary weapons alone.

Objective: Destroy the Berijev's shield generator.

With the Kurgens disposed of, Allied Command orders you to take out the Berijev's shield generator in preparation for the boarding ship. Target the Berijev and cycle through subtargets until you locate the shield generator (see Figure 8.2). Approach the vessel and spot the highlighted section to find the generator. Once again, save your secondary weapons for enemies later in the mission.

note

After 150 seconds, the Sabres automatically jump out. The consequences of not destroying them within 60 seconds remains the same whether they're killed after the time limit or simply jump out.

Figure 8.2: You must knock out the Berijev's shield generator before going after its engines.

Objective: Destroy the Berijev's engines.

The destruction of the shield generator cues your next order: disabling the Berijev by taking out its engines. Cycle through the Berijev's subtargets to locate its twin engine sections. Use primary weapons only to inflict damage. Match speed behind the Berijev so you can eliminate the highlighted sections in a single pass. Keep your shield balanced and ECM charged to defend yourself against the ship's laser turrets.

Objective: Destroy the Berijev's five laser turrets.

The Berijev's laser turrets must be eliminated to clear a path for the boarding ship. Cycle through subtargets to select the first laser turret. Divert power to your shields (if you haven't already), switch on your ECM, and activate Spectral Shields (if available) before the first attack run.

Follow your target directional indicator to locate the turret. Reduce your speed so you don't overshoot it, then open fire with your primary weapons. Cycle subtargets and use a quick burst of your afterburner, or a small nudge on the accelerator, to reach the next turret.

Objective: Destroy the Berijev's fighter escorts.

Once the Berijev's defenses are defused, the Alliance boarding ship arrives and docks with the Coalition vessel's bridge. As the marines fight their way through the ship's decks, engage any remaining Kossac fighters and keep the boarding ship safe. The marines arrive on the bridge shortly, but find no sign of the Admiral.

At the same moment, a wing of Coalition Azan fighters enters escorting an Antonov pickup ship. Watch the following cut-scene and you'll see an escape pod launching from the Berijev—the escape pod contains the Admiral!

Objective: Destroy the Antonov before it reaches the pod.

Immediately target the Antonov and use your afterburner to reach its position. The pickup ship should fall fairly quickly to your primary weapons, but if you're having trouble eliminating it, fire a couple of Hawk missiles or use some Screamers if you've equipped them.

Terminating the Antonov is only half the battle, though, as the Azan wing turns on the Admiral's pod once the ship has been destroyed. Switch targets to the nearest Azan and engage it. Work quickly, and use Hawk missiles if necessary, to protect the pod (see Figure 8.3). If you lose the pod to the Azan wing, the mission is aborted and you're ordered back to the *Yamato*.

warning

If you take too long disabling the Berijev's shield generator and engines, the Coalition Command ship jumps out and you miss the opportunity to capture an enemy Admiral. Furthermore, the mission is a failure and you're sent back to the *Yamato*.

warning

Don't let the Antonov reach the pod. Should the Antonov pick up the Admiral's escape pod, you fail the mission and are ordered back to the *Yamato*.

Objective: Protect the Nanny ship and escape pod from hostile fire.

An Alliance Nanny pickup ship enters soon after the Antonov. Keep the Azan fighters off the Nanny and work to eliminate the enemy as quickly as possible. Once the Nanny arrives, the Azan wing switches targets from the escape pod to the Alliance pickup ship.

If you failed to eliminate the Sabre wing at Nav point 1 within a 60 second time frame, an additional wing of Azan fighters enters and attacks the Nanny. Not preventing those Sabres from alerting the Coalition force means that you'll need to hold additional Hawk missiles and afterburner fuel to deal with the extra Azans.

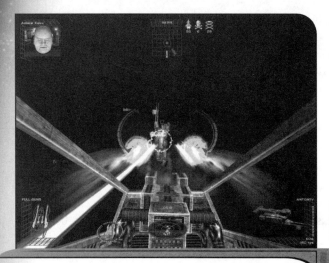

Figure 8.3: Protect the pod from fighter attack with copious amounts of Hawk missiles.

Objective: Protect the escape pod from hostile fire.

You're given the order to jump back to the *Yamato* once you've cleared the area of the Antonov pickup ship and Azan fighters. Activate your jump drive when prompted. A wing of Coalition Haidar fighters greets your arrival at the *Yamato*.

Stick close to the Nanny ship upon emerging from the jump. When the Haidar enter and attack, order your wingmen against specific ships. Target the nearest Haidar and engage it with any remaining Hawk missiles. Listen for any communiqués from the Nanny ship, and be sure to jump to the rescue if the pilot notifies you that he's taking damage from the Haidar wings.

The *Yamato* grants permission to land when the area is clear of enemy fighters.

> ## warning
>
> An additional wing of Azan fighters enters and attacks the Nanny if you failed to destroy the Coalition Warp Gate in Mission 14. Keep a reserve of Hawk missiles and afterburner fuel for the mission's end if the Coalition Warp Gate remained intact.

Mission Debriefing

 Success: Admiral Kulov's pod recovered intact.

Fail plus Kick out: Berijev escapes.

Fail plus Kick out: Pod destroyed.

Fail plus Kick out: Antonov recovers pod.

Fail plus Kick out: Nanny destroyed.

Mission 18

Mission Date: September 21, 2161

Briefing: It turns out that the Admiral we captured is Kulov himself, architect of the destruction of the French and Italian fleets. During interrogation, he revealed details of a new super gun platform, which the Coalition is about to bring online near Titan.

This weapon has the capability to destroy a capital ship with just one charge . . . a threat that must be dealt with before the gun comes online. The time window for destruction of this super gun is narrow, as a new Coalition 2nd fleet is believed to be moving in to reinforce Titan.

The *Yamato* and *Victorious* are now fitted with internal warp drives which will allow us to move directly into position near the gun platform and launch our squadrons to deal with any enemy fighters. Once the enemy fighters have been dealt with and the area is clear, the carriers will take up position and launch their torpedoes at the platform.

Ship Selection and Missile Load Out

Although you'll face several waves of Coalition fighters late in this mission, superior primary weaponry and shield and armor rating take priority over speed and mobility. Adequate armor class and plentiful ECM come in handy during your close encounter with the Coalition's super gun, Dark Reign.

The Wolverine offers the best shield and armor rating out of the three new Alliance fighters you gained access to in Mission 17. Furthermore, the Wolverine's dominant ECM rating, afterburner capacity, and Reverse Thrust ability counteract any speed and maneuverability shortcomings.

Equip the vessel with your favorite locking missile for use against the Coalition fighters later on in the mission (you'll gain more, but less damaging, missiles by selecting Hawk pods). Take along a Screamer pod if you want extra assistance in eliminating Dark Reign's stationary subtargets.

Battle Plan

Objective: Warp out to the Ion Cannon's coordinates.

Launch from the *Reliant* and await orders to activate your warp projector for the jump to the Ion Cannon's current position. Listen to your wingmen talk about the mission objectives, then proceed to the next Nav point. You'll then arrive at the Ion Cannon, known to the Alliance as Dark Reign. It appears to be inactive at first.

The *Yamato* and *Victorious* move in as you're ordered to take out the cannon's defense systems. Sadly for the crew of the *Victorious*,

warning

Dark Reign continues to charge and fire while you're eliminating its defense turrets, armor plating, and power core. Every few moments you'll hear a shot and a wingman acknowledge the loss of a Buccaneer. If you lose too many Buccaneers (meaning you're too slow in destroying the cannon), the mission fails and you're ordered to jump out.

however, Dark Reign isn't inoperable; watch the cut-scene of the powerful weapon charging and annihilating the *Victorious* Command ship in a single burst. The *Yamato* immediately pulls out to avoid destruction, and the Buccaneers are ordered against the Kurgen corvette support while the Tigers are sent to work on the Ion Cannon's fighter support.

During your battle with the Coalition fighter cover, you may come under fire from the Dark Reign tower. It's advisable to stick close to the tower, specifically near the top. If you're told Dark Reign has targeted you, immediately use the afterburner to get as close to the top of the tower as possible. Sticking close to the tower, however, will place you close to its laser turrets (see Figure 8.4). But it's safer than risking your ship against the Ion Cannon.

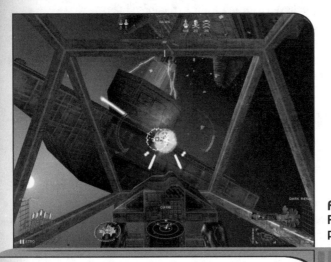

Figure 8.4: Thankfully, Dark Reign's laser turrets aren't as powerful as its Ion Cannon.

Pump up your ship's shield system (particularly if you're under attack from other fighters as well) and activate ECM to defend against the Dark Reign laser turrets or any nearby Kurgens. If you selected a ship with Spectral Shields, activate them while in close proximity to the cannon's turrets. Destroy the turrets, if you desire, to provide a safe area to hide from the powerful Ion Cannon. As you battle the turrets and fighters, Allied Command finally gets a fix on Dark Reign's shield generator.

Objective: Destroy Dark Reign's shield generator.
Dark Reign continues to blast away at Buccaneer pilots, so don't hesitate when your target switches to its shield generator. Cycle through subtargets until you locate the generator, then blow it apart with primary weapons as fast as possible. If you're taking fire from Coalition fighters, or Kurgens, balance your shields as necessary and activate Spectral Shields if applicable. Elimination of Dark Reign's

> **note**
>
> Dark Reign's shield generator actually rotates as the gun platform itself does. It might be difficult to track the subsystem if you're stationary. Consider backing off from Dark Reign and using a few missiles to eliminate the shield generator.

shield generator cues follow-up orders to destroy the armored plating that protects the cannon's vulnerable power core.

Objective: Destroy the protective panels on the power core.

You'll locate the armored plating along Dark Reign's central tube. Cycle through subtargets until you've highlighted the section. Approach and decelerate so you can destroy the protective panels in a single pass. Try to save your secondary weapons for your battle against the Coalition fighters later in the mission.

tip

While assaulting the armored plating or the power core, divert power to your shields if you're under fire from the Kurgens and/or fighters. If not, pump the power into your gun reserve so primary weapons recharge more quickly.

Objective: Destroy the power core.

Only Dark Reign's vulnerable power core remains once the armored plating has been destroyed. You shouldn't need to cycle through subtargets, as the power core should be Dark Reign's last remaining target. Remain in position after destroying the protective panels and pummel the core beneath with primary weapons (see Figure 8.5).

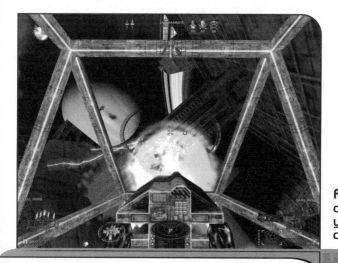

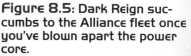

Figure 8.5: Dark Reign succumbs to the Alliance fleet once you've blown apart the power core.

The destruction of Dark Reign allows the *Yamato* to return to the mission area safely. Moments after the *Yamato* arrives, several wings of Coalition Azan and Sabre fighters enter. There's no time limit to eliminate this massive fighter attack, so take your time working your way through this final Coalition force. Order your wingmen to engage specific fighters and use the remainder of your secondary weapons (Hawk missiles are particularly effective here) until you've cleared the area of all hostile activity.

Open the communication display and ask the *Yamato* for permission to land. With the Coalition's powerful Dark Reign now just a hunk of twisted metal, the mission ends in success.

Mission Debriefing

 Success: Dark Reign destroyed.

 Fail plus Kick out: Too many Buccaneers shot down before Dark Reign destroyed.

chapter 9

The Fifth Campaign— Missions 19 to 21

The capture of Admiral Kulov and the destruction of the Dark Reign Ion Cannon mark significant victories for the Alliance. Destroying Dark Reign permitted access to Titan, and the Alliance has dropped ground troops to begin the moon's liberation.

This chapter includes detailed walkthroughs for the three vital missions that make up *StarLancer*'s fifth campaign. Plans call for the rescue of Klaus Steiner, who is being held on the prison ship *Saladin*, and an assault on the Coalition second fleet carrier, the *Varyag*, with a squadron of stolen Kamov bombers. As long as Admiral Kulov remains in custody, the Alliance should have enough momentum to push the Coalition out of the sector.

Mission 19

Mission Date: November 5, 2161

Briefing: We've just received some good news, people. Klaus Steiner, believed to have been killed in action, is alive. He is being held on a Coalition prison ship, the *Saladin*, which is currently en route to Europa. We're going to make sure she doesn't make it.

High Command wants their best on this job and has chosen us. Using the new prototype stealth fighters, we intend to rescue Steiner, along with all the other POWs in that hellhole. The Tigers will take out the *Saladin*'s fighter escort, the Scorpions, followed by the *Saladin*'s defense turrets. The *Saladin* must then be immobilized by destroying its engines, followed by its gravity drive to stop it rotating.

Once these objectives are achieved, boarding ships with Special Forces units will evacuate Steiner and the other prisoners. The final task for the Tigers is to escort the boarding ships back to Fort Bear.

Ship Selection and Missile Load Out

You're only offered one ship for this mission, the prototype stealth Shroud fighter. The Shroud is extremely maneuverable, but doesn't carry very powerful primary weapons or many missile hardpoints. Furthermore, the Shroud's lighter shield strength and armor class may require you to retreat in hectic fireballs. Its Blind Fire special ability should assist in dogfights, but watch your shield and armor strengths closely.

Its cloaking ability is the Shroud's most distinguishing feature. You can't fire primary or secondary weapons while cloaked, however, because as soon as you press either, the cloaking device deactivates and you're detectable by enemy forces.

The Shroud doesn't possess much missile loading room, so you should be selective with your choices. The protection of the boarding ship requires your utmost attention, so equip as many anti-fighter missiles as possible. Outfit the Shroud's four missile hardpoints with a mix of Hawk and Solomon pods. Conserve your missiles during the first fighter attack and the disabling of the *Saladin*—as they'll be needed once you've recovered Klaus Steiner and are making your escape.

Alternatively, you could also equip an Imp and Havoc missile to disable any fighters or Kurgens attacking the boarding ship. However, you'll only receive one warhead per hardpoint, as opposed to the three or four you'll receive with the Hawk and Solomon pods.

Battle Plan

Objective: Protect the boarding ship. Eliminate the Coalition fighter wing.

Launch from the *Yamato* in your Shroud stealth fighter. Allied Command orders the boarding ship to remain at the *Yamato* while the Tigers warp to Nav point 1 and clear out any Coalition fighter opposition. When prompted, activate your jump drive to proceed to the next mission area.

Moments after your arrival at Nav point 1, eight Coalition Haidar fighters enter. Target and engage the nearest Haidar. Though the Shroud doesn't carry powerful primary weapons, you shouldn't have much trouble against the sluggish Haidars, as it possesses a significant mobility advantage. Attempt to destroy the Haidars with primary weapons only, saving your secondary cache for use later on in the mission. Ronin wing and the boarding ship arrive at Nav point I once the Haidar fighters are eliminated. When prompted, activate your jump drive to proceed to the Coalition prison ship.

Objective: Cloak before being detected by the enemy.
Watch the cut-scene revealing the *Saladin*. Alpha wing orders the Tigers to activate their cloaking devices. Don't hesitate; toggle the Shroud's cloak immediately.

Objective: Stay cloaked until all fighters are in position.
Target the *Saladin* and cycle through its subtargets to locate its gravity stabilizers. Approach the vessel and slow down once you acquire the gravity stabilizer in your crosshairs. Don't deactivate your cloaking device or fire any weapons until ordered—if you're detected before Alpha wing is in position, the mission is flagged as a failure (see Figure 9.1).

warning

If you fail to activate your cloaking device and you enter within sensor range of the *Saladin*, the Coalition fighter escort attacks and the mission is aborted.

Listen to the communications between your fellow wingmen. As soon as you receive the signal to attack, use your primary weapons against the targeted gravity stabilizers.

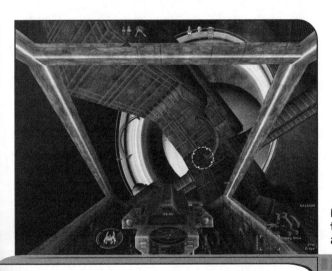

Figure 9.1: Hold position at the *Saladin's* gravity stabilizer and wait for attack orders.

Objective: Destroy the *Saladin*'s gravity stabilizers.

Destroy the first gravity stabilizer with primary weapons, then cycle through subtargets to locate the others. When you're ready, fly into position and destroy the second stabilizer, also with primary weapons. As you're within firing range of the *Saladin*'s laser turrets, be sure to divert power to your ship's shields and activate the ECM. The destruction of both stabilizers cues your orders to eliminate the *Saladin*'s turrets.

Objective: Destroy the *Saladin*'s laser turrets.

All seven laser turrets on the Saladin must be destroyed to clear the path for the Alliance boarding ship. Target the prison station and cycle through its subtargets to locate the nearest turret, then blow it up with primary weapons. You'll likely take several laser blasts to the forward shields as you attack, so divert additional power to this area and be ready with the balance-shields key. Eliminate all of the *Saladin*'s turrets to set up an attack on the remaining escort fighters.

Objective: Destroy the *Saladin*'s escort wing. Destroy the Kurgens.

With the *Saladin*'s stabilizers and turret defenses down, you're ordered to assault its fighter and a Kurgen escort. A mix of Coalition Lagg and Sabre fighters and two Kurgen corvettes remain in the mission area and must be cleared out before the boarding ship and Ronin wing arrive. Attempt to conserve your remaining secondary weapons for the final objective in the mission, by eliminating the Coalition fighters with your primary weapons. Also order your wingmen to assault the two Kurgens.

Objective: Protect the boarding ship.

After clearing the area of the Kurgens and their Lagg and Sabre fighter escorts, the boarding ship finally enters and proceeds toward the *Saladin*. Cycle through friendly targets until you've located the boarding ship, then divert power to the engines and get close (remember to match speeds here), as the vessel is about to come under attack by eight enemy Haidars!

As soon as you regain control after the Haidar fighters enter, target the nearest enemy and use your afterburner to intercept it. You don't have much time; the Haidars destroy the boarding ship within moments if you don't act quickly. Fire Solomon fire-and-forget missiles at the pack to at least disrupt its attack run against the boarding ship. Another option is to use an Imp missile (which disables their shields) followed immediately by a Havoc (which disables their electronics). The resulting explosions within the Haidar group should provide enough time to either break up the assault run or destroy them.

Once you've knocked the Haidar force down considerably, locate the boarding ship and stick close (see Figure 9.2). If the boarding ship is destroyed, the mission is flagged as a failure.

Objective: Destroy the Kurgens.

After the Haidars are destroyed and the boarding ship docks with the *Saladin*, another Coalition attack group enters with two Kurgens and a wing of additional fighters. Alliance Command scans the two Kurgens and discovers Alliance prisoners on board. While you're ordered to stay away from the corvettes at first, you're soon put in a moral dilemma as the Kurgens attack the boarding ship!

Though you're ordered against the Kurgens, don't destroy them. Instead, cycle through their vessels's subtargets and pinpoint the three laser turrets on each. Then disable the Kurgens's ability to fire

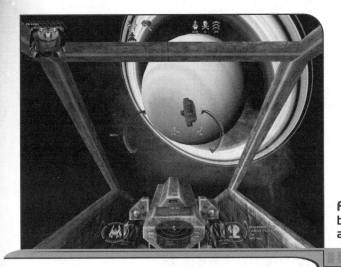

Figure 9.2: Remain close to the boarding ship during the fighter attack.

upon the boarding ship. Knock out the turrets, then return your attention to any remaining Coalition fighters. Once all enemies have been eliminated or disabled, the Alliance capital ship *Churchill* warps in with reinforcement fighters and you're ordered back to the *Yamato*.

Objective: Protect the boarding ship.

Upon your arrival back at the *Yamato*, a Coalition fighter wing known as the Scorpions enters for one last assault against the boarding ship. Among the Scorpions is the Coalition ace, Kariq Madiz. To complete the mission's bonus objective, cycle through Coalition targets until you pinpoint the one designated Scorpion Leader—that's Madiz! Destroy his fighter to complete the bonus objective.

Cycle through the remaining Coalition fighters after taking out Madiz and use any leftover missiles against them. Stay close to the boarding ship so you don't abandon it to Coalition attack. With all enemy fighters destroyed, you're ordered to return to the *Yamato* and the mission concludes as a success.

Mission Debriefing

Success plus Bonus: Madiz killed and Klaus Steiner rescued.

Success: Steiner rescued.

Fail plus Kick out: Detected by *Saladin* before signal.

Fail plus Kick out: Boarding ship destroyed.

Fail plus Kick out: Kurgens destroyed.

Mission 20

Mission Date: December 8, 2161

Briefing: Due to the recent Alliance successes, the Coalition frontline is beginning to fragment. We must seize this opportunity and hit them hard before they regroup.

A convoy has been detected trying to make a run for Coalition space. Command wants us to stop it from regrouping with other enemy ships. The convoy is made up of a Class 2 carrier, the *CS Ufelsky*, Scarab troop carriers, a Berijev command ship, and lastly an escort of heavy fighters.

Standard procedure, people. The Tigers go in first to soften up the fighters and ship defenses, then Gamma wing finishes the job with torpedoes. Once the convoy has been destroyed, return to the *Yamato*. I've also assigned the Ronin to this one, but they'll be escorting Admiral Kulov back to Alliance Command, so they won't be able to join the party.

Ship Selection and Missile Load Out

Intense dogfights dominate this mission, especially if you failed to destroy the *Rameses* in Mission 7. You'll face Kossac, Saracen, and Lagg fighters early in the mission and then battle swift and cloaking Basilisks later on in the mission. Surviving requires ample firepower, afterburner fuel, and mobility.

Select the Phoenix if you prefer using speed, acceleration, and agility (over secondary weapons) to destroy enemy fighters. Its primary weapons are quite powerful (particularly coupled with its Blind Fire special ability) and it's the only ship to feature the Nova Cannon. Pilot the Reaper if you desire enough hardpoints to equip a wide selection of anti-fighter and Basilisk missiles. The Reaper is also slightly more durable than the Phoenix, though at the expense of speed and agility.

Equip your fighter with several Hawk and Solomon pods for use against the convoy's fighter escort. Also select a few Vagabond missiles to help take out the Black Guard Basilisks. You may want to bring along a Screamer pod for use against the *Ufelsky*'s and the Berijev's laser turrets, but the hardpoint would likely best be used with additional Hawk or Solomon pods, or a Vagabond missile.

Battle Plan

Objective: Destroy the convoy and fighters.

Ronin wing, along with the transport carrying Admiral Kulov, launches from the *Yamato* moments after you do and activates their jump drives. As soon as Allied Command gives the order, activate your own drive to proceed to the next Nav point.

You'll emerge at a large Coalition fleet. Your wingmen radio to Allied Command about the situation, informing the brass that the Tigers are far outnumbered by the enemy fighters and convoy ships. They respond by sending in the Marauders. Watch the cut-scene of the Marauders entering, then target and engage the nearest fighter. The convoy's escort consists of Kossac fighters and Kurgens. Order your wingmen against specific targets, keeping them engaged with the Kossacs and well away from the convoy (see Figure 9.3).

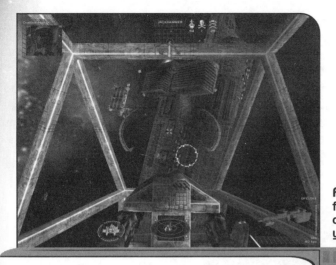

Figure 9.3: Engage the Kossac fighters away from the Coalition convoy to minimize damage to your fighter.

Objective: Take out Al Rahan (if *Rameses* was not destroyed in Mission 7).
During your battle with the Coalition Kossac fighters, the *Rameses*, last seen in Mission 7, jumps in and launches Saracen fighters, including a familiar ace pilot named Al Rahan. Of course, this takes place only if you failed to destroy the *Rameses* in an earlier mission. Obviously, the *Rameses'* presence makes the mission much more difficult. As soon as Al Rahan launches, Allied Command orders you to engage the Coalition ace.

Cycle through enemy targets until you locate the Saracen leader, Al Rahan. You can choose to eliminate him with primary weapons only, or by simply launching two or three Hawk missiles at his fighter. Once Al Rahan has been killed, continue to cycle through and destroy the remaining Coalition Saracen and Kossac fighters.

Al Rahan's Saracen isn't a very difficult target. You can handle him yourself, so keep your wingmen engaged with the other Kossacs and Saracens while you deal with Al Rahan.

Objective: Take out the Ravens.
After your engagement with Al Rahan (or, if the *Rameses* was destroyed in Mission 7 during your battle with the Kossacs), a Coalition wing of Lagg fighters known as the Ravens, led by ace Katrina Illyana, jump in and attack. Allied Command immediately orders you to attack the Ravens. Cycle through enemy targets until you locate the nearest Ravens' fighter, then assault the vessel with primary or secondary weapons.

Illyana and her squadron retreat from the mission area once either her ship has sustained significant damage, or four Ravens have been destroyed. If you're having trouble inflicting damage on the commander's ship, cycle through targets until you locate a different Raven fighter. Engage the others and eliminate four to cue their retreat.

Objective: Destroy flak turrets.

Once the Ravens jump out, Allied Command orders you to take out the flak turrets on the *CS Ufelsky* and the Berijev command ship (specifically the rear turret first). You can also accomplish this task during the early part of the mission while battling the Kossac, Saracen, and Lagg fighters.

Target the *Ufelsky* and cycle through its subtargets to locate its defense turrets. Eliminate each with primary weapons. As you approach, divert additional power to your ship's shields and activate your ECM or Spectral Shields for protection against the laser blasts. Move on next to the Berijev and cycle through its subtargets to pinpoint the location of its laser turrets. Once again, eliminate each turret with your primary weapons and keep your shields powered and balanced and ECM activated to defend yourself against the incoming fire (see Figure 9.4).

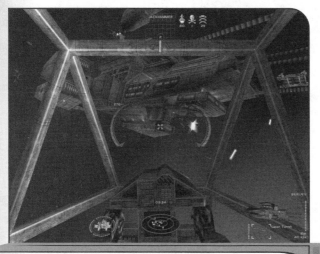

Figure 9.4: Balance your shields if you're taking damage from the Berijev's laser turrets.

The destruction of the laser turrets clears the path for Gamma wing's bombers. The Alliance torpedo bombers immediately enter and launch their warheads against the Coalition vessels.

Objective: Eliminate the Black Guard.

After Gamma wing's launch, Allied Command radios the Tigers about an emergency with Ronin wing. You're ordered to jump to their last known position and investigate. Activate your jump drive when prompted. You'll find no sign of the Ronins at their last known position, but your sensors will detect a communication beacon.

Follow the beacon's signal. The more rapid the beeping sound, the closer your ship is to it. When you reach the beacon, you'll be greeted with a message from Admiral Kulov. Apparently

note

If Gamma wing's first strike against the *Ufelsky* and Berijev fails, the Alliance capital ship, the ANS *Mitchell*, and additional bombers enter to launch more torpedoes at the Coalition convoy vessels. The mission is stamped a failure, or partial failure, should some Coalition convoy ships survive.

the Black Guard ambushed Ronin wing and recovered him. After Kulov taunts the Alliance for a few moments, Ivan Petrov and a wing of Coalition Black Guard Basilisks enter and attack. The Black Guard retreat once Petrov's Basilisk has sustained significant damage, or several of his wingmen have been destroyed.

Objective: Jump back to the *Yamato*.
Once the Black Guard retreats, Allied Command orders you to return to the *Yamato*. Activate your jump drive when prompted. Approach the *Yamato* and request permission to land to conclude the mission.

Mission Debriefing

 Success: Convoy and *Rameses* destroyed.

 Partial Success: Convoy destroyed and *Rameses* survives.

Partial Failure: *Rameses* destroyed and some convoy ships survive.

Fail: Convoy and *Rameses* survive.

Mission 21

Mission Date: December 30, 2161
Briefing: The destruction of the Ronin has been a sad loss to all of us. Intelligence believes the Black Guard was involved; let's make sure we even the score.

Alliance forces are beginning to prevail on Titan and command assures me that the moon will be secured within the week. However, it is imperative we stop the Coalition from reinforcing their ground forces on Titan with their 2nd fleet currently preparing to disembark.

Masquerading as a returning Coalition squadron, you will fly captured Kamov torpedo bombers and move through the Coalition fleet toward the flagship, CS *Varyag*. As you approach the fleet, you will be required to forward clearance codes, which are already loaded into your HUD Comms system. We have to thank Intelligence for the data and they've assured us that all codes are current.

Once the codes are accepted, you will enter the fleet in formation. Move through the outer escort ships and make your way toward the CS *Varyag*. When you are in range, launch your torpedoes at the *Varyag*. At close range with her defenses down, she should be an easy target. Once the *Varyag* is down, the Alliance carriers *Endeavor* and *Mitchell* will warp in to provide support, followed by the *Yamato*. Nanny ships will be available to rearm you with torpedoes for further strikes once the attack begins.

Stay cool on the approach, Tigers; those codes haven't failed us yet. If all goes according to plan, we will rendezvous back with the *Yamato* and launch-in fighters to join the attack. Select your fighter from the load out before launch. This will be one major battle—so watch out, it's likely to get a bit crowded out there!

Ship Selection and Missile Load Out

Though you begin the mission in a stolen Coalition Kamov torpedo bomber, you land on the *Yamato* halfway through and launch from your selected fighter to defend the Alliance Command ship from torpedo and fighter attack. Speed takes precedence over durability, as intercepting the torpedoes requires high acceleration and agility.

Pilot the Phoenix for its speed and mobility advantage over all other Alliance fighters. While it lacks missile hardpoints, its primary weapons, plentiful afterburner fuel, and Blind Fire ability make up for the lack of secondary weapons power.

Outfit your Phoenix with Hawk and Solomon pods to help take out the mission's fighter population and to intercept the torpedoes launched at the *Yamato*. You may also want to select two Jackhammer missiles to use against the *Shinnik* and *Kozlov*'s shield generators, which must be destroyed quickly to cue the *Yamato*'s attack. If you're too slow, the two Coalition capital ships jump out of the area.

Battle Plan

Objective: Jump to the Coalition 2nd fleet. Launch from the *Yamato* in the stolen Coalition Kamov torpedo bomber. When prompted, activate the Kamov's jump drive and proceed to Nav point 1 and the Coalition 2nd fleet.

Objective: Infiltrate the fleet and await clearance at the perimeter satellites.
Watch the cut-scene showing the Coalition fleet and your eventual target, the *Varyag*. An Alpha leader orders you to remain in formation and match speed with the lead Kamov. Look for the red wire frame denoting escort position, then enter it to automatically match speed with the lead ship. Or, you can simply target the lead Kamov and press the match speed button. Don't do anything that would alert the Coalition to your presence. This includes firing guns, torpedoes, or cloaking your vessel.

warning

Flying out of formation incurs the wrath of an Alpha leader, who warns you to return to position and match speed. The number of warnings you receive has a slight effect on mission outcome. However, if you're warned three times, the Coalition will discover your plan and the mission is aborted. Colliding with Coalition vessels also incites a verbal warning.

You'll reach the perimeter satellites as you approach the *Varyag*. Keep your speed matched with the lead Kamov and listen to the pilot chatter. Though it takes a moment for the clearance codes to work, you're granted access through the perimeter satellites. Follow the lead Kamov at all times as you make your approach on the *Varyag* (see Figure 9.5).

Objective: Take up position behind the *Varyag* and await orders.
Continue to follow the lead Kamov as it flies behind the *Varyag* and reaches optimum firing position. Keep your speed matched at all times so you don't overrun or collide with the vessel. Within

Figure 9.5: Remain in formation with your fellow Kamov pilots.

moments, the lead Kamov will power down its engines and reach firing position. Wait for the signal from Alpha leader to fire your warheads. If you wait too long to fire the torpedoes after being given the green light, or if your warheads miss the *Varyag*, you're ordered back to the *Yamato* to face the consequences of a failed offensive.

Objective: Make an evading course for the *Yamato*.

The *Varyag* explodes in a subsequent cut-scene if your torpedoes meet their mark. The *Yamato*, *Mitchell*, and *Endeavor* activate warp projectors and enter Nav point 1 moments after. When you regain control of your Kamov, cycle through friendly targets until you've located the *Yamato*. Divert full power to the engines or toggle on the Kamov's afterburner to reach the ship as quickly as possible. As you approach, you'll be ordered to land and switch vessels. Open up the communication menu and request permission to land.

tip

While the area will be swarming with Coalition Sabre fighters and satellite defenses at this point, ignore everything and get to the *Yamato* as soon as possible. The Kamov's poor maneuverability and primary weapons aren't very effective against the quick Sabres.

Objective: Destroy all incoming torpedoes.

You'll launch from the *Yamato* inside the fighter and with the missile load out you selected during the mission briefing. During your brief stay on the ship, the Coalition launched Kamov torpedo bombers on an attack run against the *Yamato*. Immediately press the target-nearest-torpedo button to locate any launched warheads or the nearest Kamov.

You must prevent five torpedoes from impacting on the *Yamato*. If you fail, the Alliance Command ship explodes and the mission is a failure. The number of torpedoes that hit the *Yamato* slightly affects mission outcome. Don't worry as much about the Kamovs and concentrate instead on the launched torpedoes.

Continue to cycle through torpedo targets and eliminate each warhead with either primary or secondary weapons. Match speed when trailing a torpedo so you don't overshoot or ram into the warhead. Once all of the torpedoes are eliminated, the *Yamato* orders you against the shield generators of the two Coalition 2nd fleet capital ships, the *Shinnik* and *Kozlov*.

Objective: Disable the capital ships' shield generators.

Cycle through Coalition targets until you've located the *Shinnik*. With the vessel in your sights, cycle through its subtargets until you've pinpointed the shield generator. Use your afterburner to reach the *Shinnik* as quickly as possible, then locate the highlighted section and use primary or secondary weapons to destroy the shield generator (see Figure 9.6). Though your targeting reticle then switches to the *Shinnik*'s additional subtargets, ignore the vessel for now and switch to the *Kozlov*.

warning

Work quickly against the shield generators. When you're first ordered to eliminate them, cycle the capital ship targets to see which is closer and attack that one first. If you fail to eliminate both shield generators within the time limit, the *Yamato* is destroyed by a Coalition attack and you fail the mission.

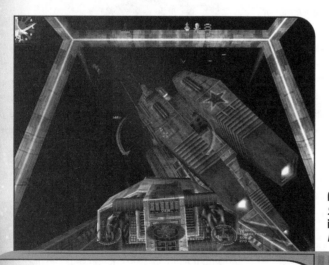

Figure 9.6: Knock out the *Shinnik*'s shield generator and immediately move on to the *Kozlov*.

Cycle through the *Kozlov*'s subtargets to select its shield generator. Use your afterburner to approach and eliminate the highlighted section with primary or secondary weapons. With both shield generators down, the *Yamato* and *Mitchell* commence their attack on the Coalition capital ships. Watch the cut-scene of the Coalition vessels exploding.

Objective: Destroy all remaining Coalition fighters and satellites.

Eliminating the *Shinnik* and *Kozlov* completes the mission's major objectives. Captain Mukai orders you to clean up the remaining Coalition force, as several Sabre fighters, satellite defenses, and Kurgens remain in the area. Order your wingmen to attack the Kurgens while you take out the fighters and satellites. You've survived this long, so don't take unnecessary risks. If you're taking too much damage from the Kurgens or Sabres, retreat with your afterburner and let your shields balance and recharge. Divert additional power to your shields if necessary and activate Spectral Shields (if available) if you're in immediate danger.

Once all Coalition ships and satellites have been destroyed, you're ordered back to the *Yamato*. Request permission to land to complete the mission with success.

Mission Debriefing

 Success plus Bonus: Only one "out of formation" warning, *Varyag* destroyed, no torpedo hits on *Yamato*, capital ships' shield generators destroyed in time.

 Success: Only one out of formation warning, *Varyag* destroyed, one torpedo hit on *Yamato* (two torpedo hits if no out of formation warnings), capital ships' shield generators destroyed in time.

Partial Success: Two out of formation warnings, *Varyag* destroyed, one torpedo hit on *Yamato* (two torpedo hits if only one out of formation warning), capital ships' shield generators destroyed in time.

Fail plus Kick out: Three out of formation warnings, *Varyag* not destroyed (took too long to launch or shots missed), five torpedo hits on *Yamato*, or take too long to destroy capital ships' shield generators.

chapter 10

The Sixth Campaign—
Missions 22 to 24

The rescue of Klaus Steiner and impressive victories against Coalition cargo ship convoys and carriers have set the stage for the final campaign of the *Yamato* and the Tigers. Provisions continue to run low, however, so before an attack on the Coalition's *Borodin* command station commences, a carefully planned assault against the *Kronstadt* supply station must be made.

This chapter includes walkthroughs for the three missions that make up *StarLancer's* sixth and final campaign. The assault against the *Kronstadt*, the base ship of the Black Guard, and the forward command station could shift the war's momentum over to the Alliance. Prepare for your toughest test yet, Tigers!

Mission 22

Mission Date: January 21, 2162

Briefing: We're damaged and low on supplies, but the Coalition's going to help us out. Captain Mukai has formulated a plan to raid a Coalition supply depot, the *Kronstadt*.

The Tigers will take the point and hit the *Kronstadt*'s early warning satellites. The next objective is to take out the *Kronstadt*'s long range comm tower; you'll have two minutes before they bypass our jamming signal. Once the comm tower is down, engage the *Kronstadt*'s fighter contingent. With the fighters out of the way, take out the *Kronstadt*'s turrets.

The depot will be left defenseless and our Rippers and light cargo ships will move in and remove the supplies. As you're well aware, this transfer process will leave the cargo ships open to attack, so we'll be providing cover in case we get unwelcome company.

With the cargo secured, Gamma wing will move in to destroy the *Kronstadt*. Your final objective will be to escort the cargo vessels to Fort Bear before jumping back to the *Yamato*.

Ship Selection and Missile Load Out

Speed takes priority over durability in a mission that features several fierce, time-intensive dogfights with Coalition vessels. Although the *Kronstadt*'s laser turrets can cause plenty of damage to lightly armored fighters, just divert power to your shields, use your ship's ECM, or select a craft with Spectral Shields. It's much more important that you pilot a fighter with topnotch agility, speed, and missile hardpoints.

The Reaper's mix of above average speed, powerful primary weapons, and plentiful missile hardpoints offers the best chance for success. If you desire slightly more velocity and additional afterburner fuel at the expense of the hardpoints, select the Phoenix. However, you can place fuel pods in one or two of the Reaper's four additional missile slots to make up for its lack of afterburner capability.

Load your missile hardpoints with Hawk and Solomon pods. You may also wish to add one or two Havoc missiles to disrupt the arrival of enemy fighters (specifically those that attack the Rippers late in the mission). Save the majority of your secondary weapons for late in the mission, as you'll need them to defend the cargo pods and Rippers from an aggressive assault.

Battle Plan

Objective: Take out early warning satellites.

After launching from the *Yamato*, activate your jump drive to proceed to Nav point 1. Coalition early warning satellites litter the area. As indicated by Allied Command, you have 60 seconds to eliminate all satellites before the system alerts the Coalition to the Alliance presence.

Knocking out the satellites is extremely difficult; it requires plenty of afterburner fuel and several hardpoints of Solomon missiles. A wingman announces the time at the 30, 15, and 5 second marks. You can attempt to order all wingmen against specific satellites, but you're unlikely to have the time (see Figure 10.1). Although failing to destroy the satellites has no direct impact on eventual mission

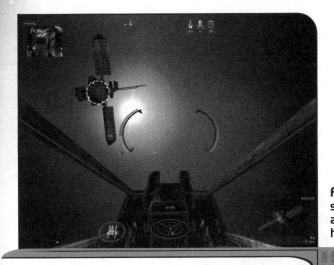

Figure 10.1: Knock out the satellites quickly to prevent additional fighters opposing you here and at the *Kronstadt*.

success, it does alert Coalition fighters into the area and adds additional fighters in defense of the *Kronstadt*.

Objective: Destroy all fighters.

If you fail to knock out the satellites in 60 seconds, a wing of Coalition fighters arrives. Once again you're on a time limit; you have another 60 seconds before the fighters jump out to alert the *Kronstadt*'s defenses of the Alliance attack. You'll need plenty of missiles (Hawks and Solomons work best) in order to eliminate all of the fighters. And although it will require plenty of afterburner fuel to engage the satellites and fighters, expending too much will make the latter portion of the mission much more difficult.

The early warning satellites and the Coalition wing impact the quantity of defenses you'll face at the *Kronstadt*.

1. If you took out the satellites in time, a wing of fighters launches from the *Kronstadt* 20 seconds after your arrival.

2. If you failed to eliminate the satellites in time, but managed to destroy the fighter wing in 60 seconds, a wing of fighters has already launched from the *Kronstadt* and is waiting for you upon your arrival.

3. If you failed to eliminate both the satellites and the fighter wing in time, you'll be greeted by two wings of fighters already launched from the *Kronstadt* and two Kurgens at the Nav point.

Objective: Destroy comm tower.

Curbing the Coalition presence at the *Kronstadt* doesn't end with Nav point 1's satellites and fighters. After jumping to the *Kronstadt*, you're ordered against its communication system to prevent further alert messages to the Coalition fleet. Depending on your performance at Nav 1, you'll face either light or heavy enemy opposition—expect wings of Haidar, Azan, and Sabre fighters, and two Kurgen corvettes in the worst case scenario.

Even if the *Kronstadt*'s defenses are plentiful, move against the comm tower as soon as possible. Target the *Kronstadt* and cycle subtargets to locate the comm tower. Approach the highlighted section and eliminate the subtarget with primary weapons (see Figure 10.2). Once the *Kronstadt*'s communications are down, engage any enemy fighters and Kurgen.

Figure 10.2: Blow apart the *Kronstadt*'s comm tower to cue the attack on its laser turrets.

Objective: Destroy the *Kronstadt's* laser turrets.

The destruction of the comm tower cues your next objective: eliminating the *Kronstadt*'s laser turrets. Take time to dogfight any remaining Coalition fighters and Kurgens in the area before moving against the turrets. Activate your ship's defensive systems as you approach the turrets, diverting power to your shields, activating your ECM, and toggling Spectral Shields (if available). Take your time with the laser turrets. If you're taking too much damage, don't hesitate to retreat and give your shields time to recharge.

Objective: Destroy cargo bay doors.

Allied Command next orders you to take out the *Kronstadt*'s cargo bay doors. Cycle through the *Kronstadt*'s subtargets until you locate its cargo doors. Destroy them with primary weapons only, saving your secondary weaponry for the remaining fighters in the mission area and additional fighters that you'll face later in the mission.

Consider eliminating all remaining Coalition fighters before destroying the *Kronstadt*'s cargo bay doors, as their removal soon signals the arrival of additional Coalition fighter wings.

Objective: Destroy all fighters.

With the cargo bay doors down, an Alliance Mammoth enters with the Rippers and begins collecting the *Kronstadt*'s cargo pods. An additional wing of Coalition fighters enters to attack the Rippers and disrupt the operation.

Objective: Protect cargo pods and Rippers.

Stick close to the Rippers and engage any incoming Coalition fighters. Save the majority of your secondary weapons to use in defense of the Rippers, as the number of cargo pods that survive determines the mission's outcome. Order your wingmen to engage specific fighters while you use your remaining Hawk and Solomon missiles against the Coalition force.

Once the Rippers complete their mission, the *Yamato* enters to finish off the *Kronstadt* with torpedoes. Jump to Fort Bear when the order comes through. Open your communication menu and complete the mission by requesting permission to land.

Mission Debriefing

 Success plus Bonus: No pods destroyed.

Success: One to three pods destroyed.

Partial Fail: Four to seven pods destroyed.

Fail: Eight to ten pods destroyed.

Mission 23

Mission Date: February 16, 2162

Briefing: This is an emergency briefing. We have found ourselves sitting about 12 clicks behind the CS *Pukov*, base ship of the Black Guard. Command wants us to eliminate it before the final push on the Coalition's forward command station, off Jupiter. I know many of you have scores to settle with the Black Guard, but stay in control—these guys are dangerous.

The first objective will be to eliminate the majority of the Black Guard, leaving the *Pukov*'s turrets open to attack. With the *Pukov*'s defenses down, the *Yamato* will engage. You will then provide cover against any fighter and bomber attacks against the *Yamato* as she moves in.

Tigers, Klaus Steiner is back with you today. He specifically requested he fly with you on this mission. We all know what happened to his unit and he knows how bad you want the Black Guard.

Ship Selection and Missile Load Out

Engaging the Black Guard and intercepting torpedoes requires an extremely agile ship loaded with missile hardpoints. Remember that one Vagabond missile (you'll want to take one with you here, as it's the best warhead against cloaking Black Guard Basilisks) requires its own missile hardpoint. The attack against the *Pukov* demands a ship with above average toughness and a high ECM rating. The Spectral Shields ability will also help achieve success.

The Shroud, despite its cloaking ability and Spectral Shields, isn't a good choice because it isn't very durable under fire and can't carry enough missiles. If you desire the Spectral Shields ability, select the Tempest; its powerful primary weapons and plentiful missile hardpoints offset its lower speed rating. Flying the Tempest requires you to equip one or two hardpoints with afterburner fuel or you'll likely run dry before the mission's final torpedo interception run.

Relying on missiles during the more difficult sections of this mission isn't a bad idea. If you desire a varied mission selection, select the Reaper for its above average speed and eight hardpoints. Speed freaks should consider the Phoenix. Though it lacks the Reaper's number of hardpoints, its speed rating and afterburner fuel provide enough mobility to track down the *Pukov*'s torpedoes.

Equip your ship with a number of Hawk and Solomon pods, but remember to take a few Vagabond missiles for use against the cloaking Black Guard fighters. Save some Solomon missiles to use against the torpedoes later in the mission.

Battle Plan

Objective: Engage the Black Guard. After launching from the *Yamato* and listening to a few communication exchanges between pilots, you're prompted to activate the jump drive to proceed to the next Nav point. Upon your arrival, you're thrown into the fire against the tough Coalition Black Guard and their cloaking Basilisk fighters.

Though the *Pukov* lies a short distance from your starting point, don't engage it. Stay away from the *Pukov* and its powerful laser turrets. After the cut-scene depicting the Black Guard launching from the *Pukov* hangar, target the nearest one and intercept. Expect a tough dogfight with each Basilisk—the Coalition ships cloak at nearly every opportunity and it's quite difficult to remain locked onto them, both with your missiles and your eyes.

tip

Vagabond missiles, with their ability to maintain a lock on a cloaked enemy and their decent damage potential, are the best choice against the Black Guard Basilisk wing. Save some Vagabonds, however. You'll need them against additional Basilisks later in the mission.

Maintain matched speed at all times while chasing a Black Guard pilot. Look for the distinct cloaked ship "distortion" while trailing the Basilisks, and continue to press the target-nearest-enemy key so you'll regain the targeting reticle as soon as the pilot decloaks. Use primary weapons to blast away the rear shielding, then launch a Vagabond missile at the exposed armor to finish the job.

Proceed through all the Basilisk fighters, attempting to stay away from the *Pukov*'s defense turrets as much as possible.

Objective: Destroy the *Pukov*'s shield generator.

With the Black Guard wing eliminated, Allied Command orders you to take out the *Pukov*'s shield generator. Target the vessel and cycle through its subtargets until you've pinpointed the shield generator. Divert full power to your shields and activate your ECM or Spectral Shields on the approach. Save your missiles for the additional fighters and torpedoes you'll encounter later in the mission and knock out the generator with primary weapons (see Figure 10.3).

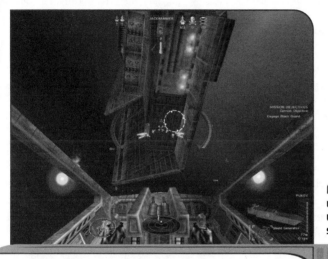

Figure 10.3: Protect yourself with Spectral Shields or ECM when attacking the *Pukov*'s shield generator.

Expect additional fighters to arrive in the area while you're dealing with the *Pukov*'s shield generator. A Coalition Sabre wing enters as well as additional Basilisk fighters. Keep your wingmen busy with the Coalition fighter cover while you handle the *Pukov*'s shield generator. Once it's down, the *Yamato* moves within range and launches Gamma wing.

Objective: Destroy laser turrets.

You must next take out the *Pukov*'s laser turrets, though this objective isn't formally announced after the destruction of the shield generator. In order for the *Yamato*'s torpedoes to hit their mark, you must eliminate more than five of the *Pukov*'s laser turrets. This is harder than it sounds, as your attention will be diverted by additional Sabre fighters and a Kamov torpedo bomber attack on the *Yamato*.

After you destroy the *Pukov*'s shield generator, hang around the ship and eliminate laser turrets until the arrival of Coalition torpedo bombers (announced by Allied Command). You should be able to knock out a few turrets while you wait. Keep the other Tigers engaged with Basilisk or Sabre fighters.

Objective: Protect the *Yamato* from Kamov torpedo attack.

Six Kamov torpedo bombers enter after the Pukov's shield generator explodes. Two of them remain stationary over the Pukov's hangar and launch torpedoes from there, while the other four immediately cloak and fly to attack positions around the Yamato. Concentrate on the two uncloaked Kamovs first. Target them by either cycling targets or by targeting the nearest torpedo, then eliminate them with primary weapons (try to save your missiles). If they've launched any torpedoes, target and destroy them before the Yamato can be damaged.

Don't bother searching for the cloaked Kamovs; you won't find them. Either move on to the remaining Coalition fighters or return to your attack on the *Pukov*'s laser turrets. During the battle, the *Yamato* reaches attack position and launches Gamma wing against the *Pukov*. You'll see the torpedoes launched during a cut-scene. Unfortunately, the bombing run fails. When you regain control, target the *Yamato* and head to its location.

Gamma wing's torpedo run fails no matter how many *Pukov* turrets you've eliminated. If you've destroyed more than five, the torpedoes impact on the *Pukov*, but have little effect. If you've eliminated fewer than five, the *Pukov*'s defensive turrets shoot down the torpedoes.

The four Kamov bombers now uncloak extremely close to the *Yamato*. If you're not in position, the *Yamato* will likely take several torpedo shots to its hull as you race to the rescue. If the *Yamato* suffers more than three torpedo hits, the Alliance Command ship jumps to Fort Bear and the mission concludes in failure.

To prevent this, intercept the launched torpedoes first, then move against the Kamov bombers. Use locking missiles, such as the Hawks, or even fire-and-forget missiles like the Solomon (they'll seek out enemy targets automatically, including torpedoes), to keep torpedoes away from the *Yamato*'s hull. Return to the Kamovs between volleys and eliminate them with primary weapons or a few missiles. The Kamovs jump out after releasing their entire payload.

Objective: Engage enemy fighters.

Additional Basilisk fighters launch after the Kamovs enter the mission area. During the entire battle with the *Pukov*'s defensive turrets and the Kamov torpedo bombers, you'll likely be diverted by remaining Sabre or Basilisk Black Guard fighters. Keep your wingmen occupied with the Coalition ships. Once the *Yamato* is safe from the Kamov torpedo attack, resume dogfighting with the Coalition fighter cover.

Objective: Protect the *Yamato*.

Once the *Yamato* and *Pukov* enter firing range, both capital ships fire successive salvos of torpedoes. Stay between both ships and press the target-nearest-torpedo key. Match speed with the torpedoes and attempt to maintain that velocity. Use your Hawk or Solomon missiles to keep the torpedoes from the *Yamato*'s hull (see Figure 10.4).

warning

The elimination of the Kamov bombers signals a last chance to take out the *Pukov*'s laser turrets. If you haven't eliminated five turrets by the time three salvos are exchanged between the *Yamato* and the *Pukov*, the *Yamato* explodes under the enemy vessel's firepower.

Figure 10.4: Hover between the two capital ships and eliminate any incoming torpedoes.

Remain midway the two capital ships, even during pauses between torpedo launches. Coalition fighters likely remain in the area, and after the second salvo of torpedoes, the *Pukov* launches another Basilisk wing. Concentrate solely on the torpedoes, and keep the rest of Alpha wing occupied with the fighters.

If you keep the *Yamato* safe from torpedo shots and have eliminated more than five *Pukov* laser turrets, the *Pukov* comes under too much fire and explodes. Request permission to land back on the Alliance Command ship and conclude the successful mission.

Mission Debriefing

 Success: *Pukov* destroyed.

 Fail plus Kick out: More than three Kamov torpedoes hit *Yamato*.

Fail plus Kick out: *Yamato* destroyed by *Pukov*'s torpedoes (fewer than five laser turrets destroyed on *Pukov*).

Mission 24

Mission Date: February 28, 2162

Briefing: The time has finally come for the assault on the Coalition forward command station. Intelligence has discovered that the command station is equipped with an ion weapon, similar to the one we encountered a few months ago that destroyed the *Victorious*. This makes a frontal assault by the *Yamato* suicidal.

We also believe that Admiral Kulov and Ivan Petrov are stationed on the base with the remnants of the Black Guard. We take them out and the Coalition is going to feel it throughout the whole sector.

This will be a two-pronged attack. The *Yamato* will launch the Tigers and Gamma wing, which will be joined by the Pirates from the ANS *Intrepid*. Using warp projectors, both squadrons will get in close to the station and begin the attack.

The Tigers' first objective is to take out the station's defensive fighters while the Pirates provide cover. Once the base's fighter defenses are clear, Gamma wing will move in and take out the station's power core and gravity drive, disabling the ion weapon. The *Yamato* and *Intrepid* will then move in and finish the job.

Ship Selection and Missile Load Out

Secondary weapons take a less important role in *StarLancer*'s final mission. The attack run against the *Borodin*, the breakaway ship, and the protection of Klaus Steiner's escape pod demands above average agility and durability, and powerful primary weapons.

Select the Phoenix as the ship best equipped to deal with the hazards of Mission 24. Its speed and agility far outclass any other available fighter with comparable firepower. Also, the Phoenix's ample afterburner fuel makes it much easier to track down enemy fighters and engage those attacking Steiner's escape pod. Should you desire to rely more on secondary weapons, select the Reaper or the Wolverine.

Outfit your ship with a few Vagabond missiles to use against the Black Guard late in the mission. Equip the other hardpoints with Hawk or Solomon pods and save them for use against any Coalition fighters attacking the Rippers.

Battle Plan

Objective: Rendezvous with the forward fleet. Warp out to the *Borodin*.

Launch from the *Yamato* and listen to the pilot chatter as you prepare to head to your final engagement with the Coalition. When prompted, activate your jump drive and proceed to Nav point 2. A cutscene depicting the formation of the Alliance forward fleet greets your arrival. Watch the scene and listen for further orders. Activate your ship's warp projector when ordered to the Coalition Command station, the *Borodin*.

Objective: Engage the defense fighters.

Several wings of Coalition Sabre and Lagg fighters welcome the Alliance attack force at the Borodin station. Allied Command orders you to engage the fighter cover as Gamma wing moves in behind the captured Coalition transport. Immediately target the nearest fighter and attack. Use the communication menu to order other members of Alpha wing against specific targets.

tip

Many defense satellites rest along the perimeter of the *Borodin* command station. Eliminate them as you battle the fighters, as terminating some of these satellites further protects the Rippers late in the mission.

Don't use all of your missiles against the initial groups of fighters—you'll face much more difficult situations later in the mission. Clear out as many fighters as you can with primary weapons. During the engagement, Gamma wing and the captured Coalition transport will reach firing range. As Gamma launches its torpedoes, the *Borodin*'s Ion Cannon comes online and rips apart both Gamma wing and the captured transport.

Objective: Destroy laser turrets on the *Borodin*.

Though Gamma launches the torpedoes in time, the warheads have no significant effect on the *Borodin* station. Allied Command reports that its scan of the station damage reveals an opened crack caused by the torpedoes' impact. New orders are to clear the way for Alliance Rippers, which will fly up, plant charges inside the opening, and detonate *Borodin* station (see Figure 10.5).

Figure 10.5: Blow apart the *Borodin*'s turrets to clear a route for the Rippers.

Target the *Borodin* and cycle through its subtargets to locate the nearest laser turret. The *Borodin*'s turrets are powerful, so enable your ship's defenses by diverting power to your shield systems, activating the ECM, or, if applicable, toggling your ship's Spectral Shields.

Objective: Eliminate any threat to the Rippers.

The *Yamato*, ten Ripper ships, and a Mammoth cargo ship carrying the explosives enter as you're destroying the laser turrets. Once twelve turrets have been taken out, the Rippers begin their approach. Listen for the Rippers' announcement that they've begun their run against the *Borodin*. Immediately after this, a wing of Coalition Sabre fighters enters the mission area near the Rippers and attacks.

tip

If any fighters remain in the area, order Alpha wing against them. If you're taking too many shots, ignore the turrets and engage the fighters yourself for a bit to decrease their numbers.

Target the Sabres (or the Rippers), activate your ship's afterburner, and set an intercept course. Of the ten Rippers that begin the attack run, four must reach the *Borodin* for the mission to proceed successfully. If less than four plant charges, you're ordered back to Nav I and greeted with the debris of what was the Alliance forward fleet. Don't hesitate to use most of your remaining secondary weapons against the attacking Sabre fighters.

If you're close to the Rippers when the Sabres enter the mission area, use a Havoc missile on the lead ship to disable several enemies. Follow up the Havoc with Solomon fire-and-forget missiles to finish off several Sabres.

Clear the area of any remaining fighters, and also destroy any stray satellites or laser turrets you might have missed earlier. With the area secure, the Rippers can acquire the explosives from the Mammoth ship and plant them in the opened crack on the *Borodin*. Once all surviving Rippers have placed their explosives, you're ordered to trigger the explosion by shooting the explosives. Back off the *Borodin* and watch the fireworks.

Objective: Prevent a breakaway ship from escaping.

The detonation causes the *Borodin* to split into several sections. Moments after the explosion, Allied Command alerts you that a piece of the *Borodin* has taken flight—Admiral Kulov is attempting an escape inside some sort of ship broken off the *Borodin*. A Warp Gate opens in front of this breakaway vessel as Coalition fighters enter. Before you can react, Klaus Steiner rams the Admiral's ship (on the warp core cover) slowing its advance toward the Warp Gate, and an escape pod jettisons from Steiner's exploding fighter (see Figure 10.6).

Figure 10.6: Klaus Steiner prevents the breakaway ship's escape with this heroic act.

Objective: Destroy the warp core on the escape section.

Allied Command orders you to eliminate the breakaway ship's exposed warp core to prevent its advance through the Warp Gate. Quickly target the *Borodin* vessel and cycle through its subtargets to the warp core. Use your primary weapons and a few missiles to eliminate the core before the breakaway ship can proceed through the Warp Gate. Concentrate solely on destroying the warp core and ignore any Coalition fighters in the area.

Objective: Protect Commander Steiner.

After the breakaway ship is either destroyed or has escaped, Allied Command launches a Nanny pickup ship and orders you to protect Steiner's escape pod until it arrives. A wing of Basilisk fighters, led by your old foe Ivan Petrov, enters while guarding Steiner's pod. Use Vagabonds and any other remaining secondary weapons against the Basilisk pilots. Stick close to Steiner's pod and eliminate any Coalition ships assaulting either the Nanny or helpless Commander. Order Alpha wing to engage the Basilisks as well.

If you don't eliminate the warp core in time, the breakaway section of the *Borodin* will jump out through the Warp Gate and you'll miss one of *StarLancer's* final cut-scenes revealing Admiral Kulov's death.

How you fare with Steiner's escape pod determines one of *StarLancer's* final cut-scenes. The Basilisk fighters jump out once Steiner is rescued or destroyed; if you manage to terminate Ivan Petrov, you'll gain another bonus cut-scene during the final sequence.

Jump to the next Nav point when prompted to return to the fleet. Watch as the *Yamato* finishes off the remaining portions of the *Borodin*. When the *Yamato* returns, request permission to land, concluding both the mission and the game.

Mission Debriefing

 Success: *Borodin* destroyed.

 Fail: Losing seven or more Rippers.

Bonus end cut-scene #1: If Admiral Kulov was destroyed in breakaway ship before it entered the Warp Gate.

Bonus end cut-scene #2: If Petrov was destroyed with the Black Guard.

Bonus end cut-scene #3: If Klaus Steiner was killed in his escape pod.

Bonus end cut-scene #4: If Klaus Steiner's escape pod was rescued.

part 4

Multiplayer Combat

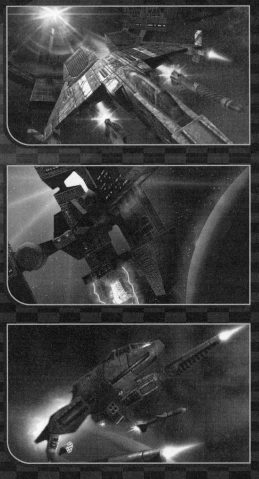

Surviving against the computer-controlled Coalition pilots is one thing—succeeding against highly skilled human opponents is another! Dominating other human pilots, either alone or as part of a *StarLancer* cooperative squadron, requires specialized strategies and techniques only offered here, in "Part 4—Multiplayer Combat."

Chapter 11 takes the skills that you've gained from combat training and the single-player game and applies them to deathmatch warfare. Here you'll learn the fundamentals of defeating a crafty human opponent, either in one-on-one or free-for-all situations. A complete rundown of the multiplayer game types and power-ups are included along with expert strategies for each.

Chapter 12 offers strategies for successful cooperative missions. You'll learn the basics of effective team communication, combined attacks, and target selection.

chapter 11
Deathmatch Strategies

Human adversaries offer an unpredictable challenge. While you may discover patterns in a computer-controlled ship's behavior, you can never be sure what a human pilot will do next. You may have the human player in your crosshairs only to lose him to a burst of afterburner fuel. You may be trailing close behind only to get a proximity mine dropped at your ship's nose. This unpredictability keeps multiplayer gaming fresh and exciting.

This chapter examines *StarLancer*'s intense world of multiplayer deathmatches. While most of the basic single-player strategies you learned from flight and combat training apply here, every aspect is turned up a notch. Refer to this chapter for tips on ship selection, a rundown of the multiplayer power-ups, and strategies for each deathmatch arena.

Deathmatch Dogfighting

Succeeding in dogfights against human opponents over a local area network or against the seasoned human space combat pilots over Microsoft's Internet Gaming Zone requires intimate knowledge of the *StarLancer* game. This section covers the skills required to battle the best human fliers in one-on-one dogfights.

Ship Selection

Before heading out to the deathmatch arena, it's important to take care during the ship selection process, as this process allows players to differentiate themselves from their opponents. As you've seen in Chapter 3, "Ship Strategies and Statistics," each *StarLancer* fighter carries unique abilities. Be sure and select the ship that best suits your unique style of dogfighting (see Figure 11.1).

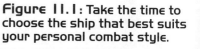

Figure 11.1: Take the time to choose the ship that best suits your personal combat style.

If you're adept at ship maneuvers and the use of primary weapons, select a more agile fighter at the expense of durability. If you're not highly skilled at outmaneuvering enemy fighters, you might want to select a more durable fighter at the expense of mobility, and use your hull strength and the acquisition of power-ups to provide an edge against your opponents. Ship selection is also heavily dependent upon the specific deathmatch arena that you'll be playing in. For more on the available arenas, head to the "Deathmatch Arenas" section later in this chapter.

Use the ship's power distribution system to offset any potential weaknesses. For instance, if you prefer an agile fighter with lower shield strength, consider diverting additional power from the guns or engines to the shield recharge system. Likewise, if you're piloting a more durable craft, divert power from the shields to engines in order to increase speed or the primary weapon recharge rate.

Below are some suggestions on multiplayer ship selection and details on how each ship caters to a different style of play.

 Mirage: A solid balance of agility and durability, the Mirage offers some of the most destructive primary weapons around. Though it lacks special abilities, its powerful guns should always keep you in the fight.

 Patriot: An excellent dogfighting ship equipped with decent primary weapons and the Blind Fire ability, the Patriot lacks durable hull armor. Its Blind Fire feature, though, provides a considerable edge in battles that occur in close quarters. You may need to keep shield energy recharged by diverting power away from guns or engines.

 Phoenix: The Phoenix excels in primary weapons and mobility. Couple its dogfighting prowess with its Blind Fire and Reverse Thrust abilities and you have an efficient fragging machine. Keep shields charged to offset its power armor and don't forget to use the Nova Cannon!

 Shroud: The fastest fighter in the Alliance fleet, the Shroud can outmaneuver all other ships, but its weak primary weapons will cause problems. However, equipped with Blind Fire, Reverse Thrust, Spectral Shields, and Cloaking ability, the Shroud shouldn't be overlooked (see Figure 11.2).

 Reaper: A durable ship with an extremely fast rate of primary weapons fire, the Reaper lacks some mobility compared to other ships. Divert power away from the shield system to the engines in order to boost speed.

 Wolverine: Powerful primary weapons and heavy armor balance the Wolverine's poor acceleration and dexterity. Keep abreast of the power distribution system and divert energy to the engines as necessary. The Wolverine's Reverse Thrust ability will allow you to perform some fancy maneuvers, particularly when escaping attackers.

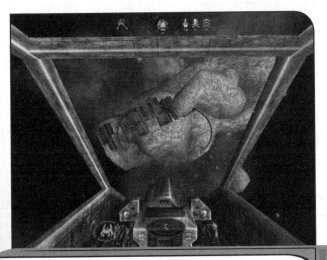

Figure 11.2: The Shroud's speed comes in handy during the Nuclear Threat scenario—get through that gate fast!

Power-Ups

Scattered around each deathmatch arena are glowing orbs that, when picked up, affect your ship in some manner. Ships only begin deathmatch games with standard lasers, so it's important to snag power-ups early and often in order to gain an edge on your opponents. Keep in mind that all of these glowing orbs appear the same on-screen— so, you won't know which power-up the orb represents until you've grabbed it!

Observing a player as he snags a power-up can help you adjust your strategy. For instance, if your opponent's ship slowed down suddenly after grabbing the power-up, you can assume they grabbed the Half-Max Speed "bonus." Or, if your opponent's ship Cloaked, you can assume that he just grabbed the Cloak power-up. Watch the ship's behavior after snagging the power-up and become more aggressive or more defensive accordingly.

tip

As most deathmatch players will hang around the arena's greatest concentration of power-ups, this area provides a great spot to set up an ambush. Predict their maneuvers toward the power-ups and fire your primary weapons at the orb itself. This way you'll inflict damage to their ships as your opponents attempt to collect their rewards.

Detailed below are the power-ups you'll encounter in each deathmatch arena and how best to utilize them. Note that you can only activate one power-up at a time. For example, if you collect a Missile boost you must fire it before grabbing another power-up.

Countermeasure: Snagging a Countermeasure power-up adds three decoys to your ship's inventory. Save the decoys for missile locks and use them as you would during the campaign game. Supplement your decoy use with the afterburner and quick turns to evade an enemy player's missile.

Fuel: Afterburner fuel is a coveted commodity in multiplayer games—you'll likely never have enough! Many of the power-ups you capture will add additional fuel to your ship's reserves.

Half-Max Speed: Classified as a "power-down," the Half-Max Speed decreases your ship's maximum velocity for a limited amount of time. You'll still be able to use your afterburner reserves, but it's best to stay away from enemy players while hindered by this power-down.

Invulnerability: Procuring an Invulnerability power-up makes your ship indestructible for a short period of time. You can't be destroyed, so aggressively attack other ships. Don't hesitate to approach the opposing ships and even ram their hulls!

Missile: No ships carry missiles by default in multiplayer—you have to grab them via power-up! As Missile power-ups are scarce, save them for close encounters with enemy human players. Use them to weaken an enemy ship's shields and/or as a precursor to an assault with your primary weapons.

Proximity Mine: One of the most mischievous power-ups, the Proximity Mine can be dropped out of your ship's rear with the fire-missile button. It's a perfect counter when you've got an enemy ship on your tail! Ramming the Proximity Mine almost always destroys the victim (see Figure 11.3).

Figure 11.3: Grab the power-ups to pick up a Proximity Mine.

 Repair: If you're heavily damaged, start grabbing power-ups as fast as possible. If you're lucky enough to find a Repair orb, your ship's shields and hull armor will be restored.

 Reverse Yoke: Another "power-down," grabbing a Reverse Yoke will reverse the direction of your ship's pitch and yaw controls, making it extremely difficult to maneuver.

 Shields Down: Flying over the Shields Down power-up disables your ship's shields for a limited amount of time—not a good situation in a heated deathmatch game! Use your afterburner to flee from any attackers as you're much easier to kill without shield protection.

 Ship Cloak: Offers limited-time invisibility, though you will become visible if you fire any weapons. Use the Cloak to sneak up on unsuspecting ships and pummel them with primary weapons or a missile.

Deathmatch Arenas

StarLancer offers several specially-designed arenas for free-for-all and team deathmatch play. Though you'll find power-ups in each arena, the layouts and objectives change considerably. All of the deathmatch arenas have restricted, predefined battle areas. If you try to fly past these boundaries, your ship will bounce off and return into play. Most of the action takes place around the heavy concentration of power-ups. Venturing away from the action might keep you safe, but it certainly won't help you rack up kills.

In this section you'll find strategies for *StarLancer*'s deathmatch arenas, including tactics for both free-for-all and team-based combat.

Asteroid Field

Objective: A no-frills arena set in a dense pocket of asteroids where the only rule is survival of the fittest. In Asteroid Field team play, the team with the most frags wins.

Cluttered with gigantic space boulders, the Asteroid Field deathmatch arena is an extremely tight battleground with not much room to maneuver. Therefore, speed isn't as important as durability. Choose a ship that excels in both armor and shield strength as well as primary weapons (the Reaper and Wolverine are fine choices), and use the power distribution system to offset any speed deficiencies.

As with any deathmatch arena, use the environment to your advantage. The asteroids can be used both offensively and defensively. For instance, if you can't shake an enemy player off your tail, head directly for an asteroid and make a sharp turn around the rock, hopefully causing your opponent to smash into the asteroid. Also, use the asteroids as cover against enemy fighters. Hide behind them to allow your ship's shields to recharge or use the shield of the asteroids as a safe spot from which to locate new power-ups or ambush passing fighters (see Figure 11.4).

Figure 11.4: Asteroids make for great cover when you need to take a breather.

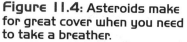

Do everything in your power to keep from ramming into the asteroids. Should you strike one, work quickly to balance your shields, and consider diverting additional power to the shield system in order to recharge faster. You're in a highly vulnerable spot after ramming an asteroid, having taken heavy damage to both shields and hull. You likely aren't moving very fast either, which makes you an easier target for an enemy's primary weapons.

Dark Reign

Objective: An arena built around an active Dark Reign gun tower. The player who finds the power core is immune from being targeted, while it's still open season on the others. All kills by the Dark Reign are added to the controlling player's score. In Dark Reign team play, the entire team controlling the gun tower is immune to targeting.

If you played through *StarLancer*'s single-player campaign, you'll instantly recognize the imposing Dark Reign. The cylindrical-shaped tower locks on specific fighters and fires a powerful ion beam at the designated target. A solid strike from the tower will easily destroy any Alliance fighter.

Don't necessarily feel compelled to hunt down the power core immediately. Though you're protected from Dark Reign's beam attacks, you still might fall behind in the scoring table if the other players are fragging each other away from the tower. Seek out the power core, but be sure to target other fighters as well. You can't count solely on Dark Reign to score kills for you.

tip

If you managed to locate the power core and have pursuers, hang around the Dark Reign. At close range, the tower should have little trouble targeting your attackers and adding to your kill score.

Hunt the Shadow

Objective: In Hunt the Shadow, the first player to frag an opponent plays the Shadow. The Shadow is indefinitely cloaked and is able to pick off the other ships, but has no shields and cannot acquire power-ups. The player who destroys the Shadow gets five frags for his efforts and is next to don the cloak. In Hunt the Shadow team play, the team with the most frags wins.

Hunt the Shadow takes place around a derelict base installation and a surrounding small asteroid belt. Power-ups are mainly scattered inside a tunnel that runs through the base, though you'll also find some power-ups near the bottom and top of the installation.

If you plan to make successful attacks with the shadow, you'll need a ship with powerful primary weapons and durable hull armor. Without shields and the ability to snag power-ups, you're basically defenseless in a battle without excellent guns and armor. Furthermore, a ship with Spectral Shields can help protect your exposed hull during intense dogfights. Select the Crusader, Reaper, or Wolverine for your best chance of survival as the Shadow.

warning

With so many places to hide, it's not difficult for the Shadow to stay concealed for minutes at a time. Keep in mind that while it's fun being the Shadow, you won't increase your kill count if you're hiding for the duration of the game.

As the Shadow, hide behind the installation or asteroids and look for opportunities to get behind unsuspecting fighters or to ambush players engaged with one another. If attacked as the Shadow, retreat to the installation or asteroids to shake the enemy, then resume waylaying your foes.

If you're searching for the Shadow, look for the cloak's distinctive distortion against the blackness of space. Keep the cloaked vessel in your crosshairs and try to hold the Missile power-up for when you spot it. One warhead should severely damage the shieldless Shadow.

Nuclear Threat

Objective: Strewn amongst a small field of asteroids are six beacons. The player who can collect all six and fly through the beacon gate will trigger a nuclear strike killing all other players in the blast. Destroying a player's ship will scatter any beacons he's carrying.

At the start of Nuclear Threat, the six beacons (which look like white power-ups) are scattered throughout the arena behind asteroids and other debris. Collecting all six is a lofty goal, so don't expect to be able to locate them all before other ships scoop some up. Instead, play Nuclear Threat as you would a standard deathmatch, but be sure to accumulate any beacons you come across. Search the explosions of any fighters you destroy and grab any discarded beacons.

Attack aggressively if you aren't carrying a beacon or only have a few. Use the power distribution system to divert more power to guns and engines. As you begin to accumulate the devices, be sure to fly more defensively. Divert more power to the shield system and retreat from battles to grab power-ups or to recharge shields.

Quick, yet powerful, ships work well in Nuclear Threat. Go with the Phoenix, Reaper, Patriot, or Mirage for excellent results. The Shroud could excel through its cloaking and speed alone, but its weak primary weapons pose problems. If you manage to collect all six beacons, make a dash for the beacon gate, which spins in the arena's center. Divert additional power to the engines and use afterburner fuel (see Figure 11.5).

Figure 11.5: With all six beacons in your cargo hold, fly through the beacon gate to initiate the nuclear blast.

Tag Bomb

Objective: Each player's ship is fitted with a 45-second time bomb in the Tag Bomb arena. The first ship fragged will respawn with their timer ticking down. If the player with the active bomb collides with another player, his bomb will stop ticking and the other player's will start. If a player is destroyed by his bomb, the person who tagged the player will get two frags instead of one. In Tag Bomb team play, the team with the most frags wins.

The bomber icon and timer countdown appear at the top of the ship's HUD. If you're the first ship fragged, or you're tagged by the bomber, the timer starts to count down. To stop the timer, you must tag another ship by colliding with it. Getting killed is the only other way to stop the timer.

Don't feel threatened by the bomb aspect too much. You can still rack up kills normally by improving your ship through power-ups and dogfighting opponents. If the bomber tags your ship, however, stop trying to shoot down other players with primary weapons and divert all power from the gun systems and some from the shields system to your engines. Target the near-

> **tip**
>
> Keep tabs on the current bomber as much as possible. Gauge its current speed, distance, and damage level by cycling through enemy targets until you've pinpointed its location. Stay away from the bomber and engage other players elsewhere in the arena.

est fighter and intercept it with afterburners. It's especially easy to collide with ships already engaged in battle; players currently in combat often ignore the approaching bomber.

Fleeing from the bomber requires speed. If your ship outpaces the bomber's craft, you shouldn't have a problem. Choose a fast, but formidable ship (such as the Phoenix, Patriot, or perhaps the Shroud) at the selection screen. If you stay alert and keep your finger ready on the afterburner, it's unlikely that you'll ever be tagged.

All excellent dogfighting ships work well in Tag Bomb. Durable hull armor or better shielding won't protect you from getting tagged or from the bomb's detonation. Select the ship you're most comfortable with, make sure it possesses powerful primary weapons, and then use the power distribution system to offset any weaknesses.

Vampires

Objective: The first blood of the match becomes the first Vampire. Vampires can spread their disease by killing an uninfected player. The last player left will score five frags, and all players will then be cured of their affliction and the process starts over. Vampires cannot pick up power-ups.

The goal of the Vampires arena is to be the last player alive—or in this case, the last player uninfected! Unlike some variations of this game style, if you're killed you can return to battle, though you're hindered slightly by your subsequent inability use power-ups. Thus, any remaining uninfected ships carry a slight advantage over the Vampires.

Vampires operates similarly to a standard deathmatch, but the five bonus frags awarded to the last uninfected player add up considerably. If you're infected, the chance of scoring consistent kills drops dramatically. Don't expect to lead the kill board if you're constantly a Vampire.

Staying alive requires much more defensive thinking than is required in a straight-up deathmatch. After battles, you should retreat and allow your shields to balance and recharge. Also, spend time between combat collecting power-ups to gain afterburner fuel, repair your ship, grab missiles, or acquire a special ability like invulnerability or cloaking. If you stay back (or what some players refer to as "camping"), the Vampires might "infect" the remaining players (see Figure 11.6). By the time you're discovered, you could already be the last uninfected player and gain the five bonus frags!

tip

If you're uninfected and have the choice of ambushing an uninfected player or a Vampire, always choose the uninfected player. Killing either awards you the same amount of frags, but dogfighting the Vampire puts you at risk of infection.

Figure 11.6: Uninfected and hanging out behind this asteroid waiting for the chance to be number one.

chapter 12

Cooperative Strategies

B attling the Eastern Coalition alongside friends and other *StarLancer* players from around the world provides an entirely different experience from the solo campaign. Though the missions remain relatively similar to the single-player game (you can expect tougher enemies in larger quantities), the teamwork required to successfully complete each episode demands competent communication, situational awareness, and an efficient chain of command.

In this chapter, you'll find tactics specific to *StarLancer*'s cooperative multiplayer game. Each of the single-player missions can be played online, over a network, or through modem and serial connections with up to four players total. Conquering the Coalition as a team requires special strategies. Search the following pages for tips on ship selection, delegation of duties, team communication, and strategies for specific mission types and situations.

Cooperative Teamwork

Team games are extremely popular, so it's little surprise that a cutting-edge game like *StarLancer* offers a full cooperative campaign mirroring the single-player game. To operate effectively as a team, players need to plan ahead, make careful ship and mission choices, and be aware of each other's actions during the course of the mission.

This section details the specific strategies for pre-mission planning and the mid-mission communication vital to any *StarLancer* cooperative team.

Ship and Missile Selection

Tackling missions as a team begins at the ship and missile selection screen. Just as you would in the single-player campaign, carefully consider your choices here and be sure that each ship and missile selection is appropriate for the job at hand. By selecting ships and missiles that cater to a particular team member's duty and strength, you can maximize the team's potential for success (see Figure 12.1).

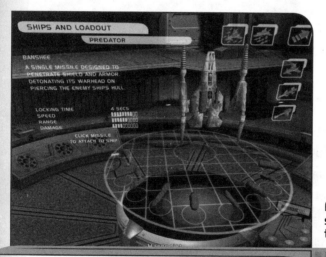

Figure 12.1: Team members should select ships and missiles that complement one another.

Don't allow each team member to select identical fighters and missile load outs, as this will prove counterproductive. Each *StarLancer* mission includes several objectives to complete and each flier will often require a different ship, missile, or even plan of attack. For example, in a capital ship or base assault mission, the fighter that assaults the base should hold a different missile load out than the fighter or fighters sent to engage enemy fighters or Kurgen corvettes providing cover.

Be sure to select ships and missiles that complement one another. Place some team members in heavier, more durable, ships for capital ship, base, or Kurgen encounters. Equip them with powerful Jackhammer warheads as well as Screamers or standard anti-fighter missiles. Players assuming dog-fighting duty should pilot fast, agile fighters with adequate primary weapons and Blind Fire ability.

They should also be fully loaded with anti-fighter missiles such as the Bandit, Raptor, Hawk, or Solomon. Team members taking on the role of enemy torpedo interception should focus on speed above other considerations.

Chain of Command

Another way to promote cooperative success is to designate a team leader to concentrate primarily on staying on top of current mission and situational conditions. For instance, the team leader would pay close attention to all directives from Alliance Command, including altered mission objectives and incoming Coalition fighter or bomber announcements. The leader could then delegate team member duties and make adjustments according to current conditions.

If you do form a chain of command, it's important for all team members to adhere to that chain during the course of the mission. If team members start ignoring orders and issuing their own commands, the structure breaks down and it will be much harder to successfully and efficiently complete mission objectives. With the team leader focused on current mission conditions, the members are free to concentrate solely on performing their designated duty. If the system collapses, torpedoes could be missed, targets could be neglected, and objectives will almost certainly not be met.

tip

If you're playing online with players you don't know personally, be friendly and don't automatically assume the leadership role. Proclaiming yourself instant leader could alienate you from the rest of the team. A team that gets along well performs much better in battle!

Team Communication

Failure to communicate effectively during a cooperative mission can cause the entire sortie to fall into shambles regardless of pre-mission preparation. If you're to succeed in *StarLancer*'s cooperative multiplayer missions, either with friends or unknown allies online, you must communicate during the mission. Keeping other team members abreast of the current situation is crucial.

Good communication involves alerting teammates of current mission conditions, such as the primary target, the amount of fighter cover, and the presence of bombers or torpedoes. It's also important to speak often when

tip

Whichever abbreviations or shortcuts you decide upon, be sure to notify all team members beforehand (a good location would be the pre-mission chat lobby). Effective teamwork relies on each pilot possessing similar knowledge about communication and the plan of attack. Any disruption could cause orders to go awry and lead to costly mistakes.

engaging any type of enemy. If you're going to handle the remaining three Coalition fighters, be sure to tell your team. If you plan to assault the capital ship, notify the others so your wingmen can engage the ship's fighter cover (see Figure 12.2).

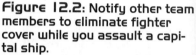

Figure 12.2: Notify other team members to eliminate fighter cover while you assault a capital ship.

An intense, fast-paced action game, *StarLancer* doesn't offer much down time for extended communication; therefore, you should create convenient shortcuts. Examples include abbreviating "Front" and "Rear" to "F" and "R" and "Left" and "Right" to "L" and "R" to provide directions when giving orders. Additionally, you can create abbreviations for the names of Coalition fighters and capital ships. For instance, try abbreviating Azan to "Az" and Haidar to "Hai." The team leader can alert fellow pilots that "8 Az in," meaning eight Coalition Azan fighters are incoming. Anything that cuts down on the amount you need to type will help.

Mission Strategies

Adequately preparing for a cooperative mission is one thing; actually performing well in tense situations and as a team provides its own particular challenges. Each sortie poses new problems and a team must plan in advance how to approach different circumstances.

In this section you'll find situational strategies for *StarLancer*'s main mission types. Though each mission isn't covered in specific detail, the following tactics will prepare you for nearly every type of situation you'll face during the campaign.

Escort and Defend Missions

Escort missions require protection of critical craft, such as cargo vessels or a civilian capital ship, against often overwhelming odds. The Coalition rarely holds anything back. If you're ordered to protect a valuable Alliance craft, you can expect the Coalition to send several wings of fighters, Kamov bombers, and Kurgen corvettes to ensure that you don't complete your mission.

On a four-pilot team, delegate at least two fighters to torpedo and bomber interception duty. Select the fastest, yet still powerful, fighter available at the time. Pilot the Predator or Naginata early in the campaign, then switch to the Coyote or Patriot during the middle and later sections. Fighters with Blind Fire (such as the aforementioned Predator, Coyote, and Patriot) prove extremely effective against torpedoes. Equip plentiful anti-fighter locking missiles, as the warheads are equally effective against incoming torpedoes.

The cooperative multiplayer missions feature the same order, structure, and goals as the single-player campaign, but you'll face additional enemy ships. Head to Chapters 5 through 10 for complete walkthroughs of all the single-player missions.

Players ordered to intercept torpedoes should ignore all other targets and concentrate solely on the incoming missile threat. Divert most of your ship's power to the engines if you're running low on afterburner fuel; otherwise, use the afterburner generously. One member of the anti-torpedo team should attempt to engage the enemy bomber(s) while the other intercepts the torpedoes (see Figure 12.3).

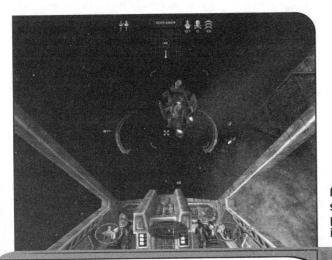

Figure 12.3: One team member should attack the Kamov torpedo bombers while another intercepts the warheads.

The other team member and the leader should concentrate on any Coalition fighter or Kurgen support craft. The two pilots should stick close to the critical Alliance vessel and intercept any torpedoes missed by the anti-bomber group. These pilots should launch in the best dogfighting fighters available, which can vary depending on your personal taste. Make sure that you select a ship with ample missile hardpoints in order to equip many locking missiles, though. If required, equip one dogfighter with Jackhammers, to deal with the Kurgen, and Havoc or Imp missiles to use against an incoming cluster of enemy fighters.

Patrol and Dogfight Missions

Ship selection for fighter-heavy missions depends on a player's personal preference. Some prefer a durable, but slower ship with emphasis on powerful primary weapons over plentiful missile hardpoints. Then again, others enjoy faster, more agile ships at the expense of durability and firepower. Place each player in the best available dogfighting ship that's both effective and comfortable.

Mission selection is also key for dogfight missions. For optimum success, two pilots should launch in fighters containing ample missile hardpoints (ample meaning more than five) and equip as many anti-fighter missiles as possible. Other pilots can specialize. Havoc and Imp missiles work especially well against clusters of incoming fighters, with the former disabling electrical systems and the latter taking out shield systems.

Communication plays a large role in dogfight situations, particularly if one player becomes overwhelmed by Coalition vessels. Listen for commands or pleas for assistance from your wingmen. If a team member asks for help, cycle through friendly targets to locate his

> **tip**
>
> If you expect to encounter the Coalition Black Guard, who pilot cloaking Basilisk fighters, be sure to equip some team members with Vanguard missiles. Vanguards retain a target lock even if enemy fighters engage a cloaking device.

or her position. Then intercept and engage the Coalition fighters attacking your wingman. Conversely, if you're the one stuck inside a cluster of enemy fighters, use your afterburner to escape, balance shields as needed, and open the communication display to radio for assistance.

Capital Ship and Base Assault Missions

Assaulting Coalition capital ships and bases can be handled in a manner similar to escort and defend missions. The team should be split into two primary attack groups. Half of the team should concentrate on the capital ship or base itself, while the other half engages the Coalition fighter cover.

Ship selection is highly dependent on your assigned duty. Attacking a capital ship or base at close range requires a durable ship with good shield strength and hull armor ratings. Furthermore, plentiful ECM and Spectral Shields offer additional protection against the Coalition's damaging laser turrets. The assaulting team should also consider primary weapon strength over missile hardpoints, as it's easier to destroy each subtarget with close range primary weapons than waiting for missile locks (see Figure 12.4). However, if you prefer missiles, select Screamer pods, each of which offers twenty dumbfire missiles that are highly effective against slow-moving and immobile targets.

Remaining team members should pilot preferred dogfighting craft and engage the Coalition fighter cover. Their primary goal is to keep enemy fighters off the capital ship or base assault team. Equip the dogfighters with anti-fighter missiles and consider mounting a few Jackhammer missiles for use against Kurgen corvettes.

The assaulting group should remain in communication at all times during the mission, particularly when ordered against the capital ship or base. Good communication prevents the assaulting group from attacking the same target or subtarget. For instance, when taking out laser turret

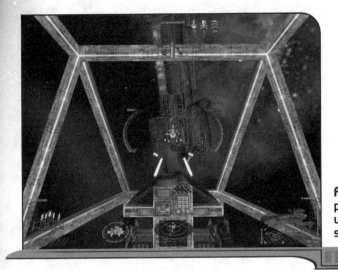

Figure 12.4: Select a ship with powerful primary weapons to work through a capital ship's subsystems quickly.

subtargets, order one member against the front section and the other against the rear section. Careful delegation of targets will save time and prevent unnecessary doubling up.

appendix A
Medals

Every *StarLancer* pilot strives to receive all eleven campaign and valor medals. It takes determination, practice, and knowledge to acquire each award. Read on to obtain the information you'll need to secure all of the medals available in *StarLancer*.

This appendix compiles the complete list of campaign and valor medals you can attain during *StarLancer*'s single-player game. Campaign medal descriptions include mission dates, conflict position, and the current Alliance–Coalition situation that governs the issuing of the medal. Valor medal descriptions include objectives required and the mission in which the medal can be received.

Campaign Medals

As you might expect, campaign medals are awarded upon the completion of *StarLancer*'s campaigns. While excelling in each of the campaigns certainly helps your score, you need only complete the campaign to receive a reward. Each medal is awarded before the mission that begins the next campaign.

Alliance Defense Mobilization Medal

Campaign Phase: June 2160–September 2160

Operational Position: The Triton Quadrant, forward positions off Neptune

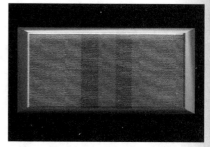

This campaign medal is awarded for the long and desperate retreat of the fleeing Alliance vessels scattered across the Solar system after the initial Coalition attack. The 45th Squadron plays a vital role in protecting these escaping vessels, both military and civilian, as they head for the relative safety of the Alliance's new Command base, and rallying point, at Triton— Neptune's largest moon.

Long-range Forces Commendation Medal

Campaign Phase: October 2160–February 2161

Operational Position: The Triton–Uranus Quadrant

The 45th and the *Reliant* continue their operations to escort and protect incoming vessels to the relative safety of the Alliance's rallying point around Triton. However, their actions have been expanded to hit-and-run missions on Coalition military targets. The campaign medal is awarded for weakening Coalition forward hunting packs in an effort to fend off any attempts to strike the new Alliance Command base.

The secondary objective of this campaign is to attack strategic Coalition targets and secure much needed supplies and technologies for the Alliance by raiding enemy bases and facilities. The 45th's reputation begins to grow and they become known as "The Flying Tigers." During this campaign, the 45th Squadron plays its part in disrupting the development of the Coalition Warp Gate facilities as well as a super carrier construction base. The Flying Tigers also manage to secure coding and warp technology, which will later enable the Alliance to hit-back at the Coalition.

Special Operations Service Medal

Campaign Phase: March 2161–July 2161

Operational Position: The Triton–Saturn Quadrant, forward positions between Neptune and Saturn

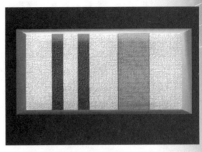

Having failed to annihilate the Alliance with its hunting packs, Coalition forces withdraw to the quadrants around Titan in order to regroup. However, the Coalition has developed an Advanced Warp Gate facility to ambush Alliance vessels from long-range.

    Alliance forces still operating between Neptune and Saturn have been able to regroup much of their remaining military strength and resources over the last two campaigns. Here, the Alliance begins the first phase of their counter attack, and prepares for the liberation of Titan. The campaign medal is awarded for destroying the Coalition's Advance Warp Gate facility. Additional objectives include mounting surprise attacks and ambushes to weaken the Coalition's forward fleet around Titan.

Joint Services Commendation Medal

Campaign Phase: August 2161–September 2161

Operational Position: The Triton–Saturn Quadrant, holding position off Saturn and Titan

This campaign medal is awarded for the capture of Admiral Kulov, the first Coalition Admiral to be apprehended by the Alliance. It is hoped that information from Kulov will help secure Titan's early liberation. The destruction of the Coalition Ion Cannon—that threatened the Alliance's advance to free Titan—allows the dropping of troops to the planetary surface. The land war for the liberation of Titan has begun.

Battle of Titan Campaign Medal

Campaign Phase: October 2161–December 2161

Operational Position: The Triton–Saturn Quadrant, forward positions off Saturn and Titan

The operations in this campaign involve the tracking and destruction of the 2nd Coalition forward fleet as it tries to reinforce its ground troops. Alliance forces prevail and drop troops, finally securing Titan.

The campaign medal is awarded for the destruction of the 2nd Coalition forward fleet. This allows the Alliance to complete its staging base off Titan and advance to the next strategic phase of the war: the liberation of Jupiter and its colonies.

Valor Medals

Valor medals are awarded for specific acts of heroism, often involving a mission's bonus objectives. Acquiring the valor medals requires elite piloting skills and a focused obedience to the mission objectives.

Follow the mission walkthroughs outlined in "Part 2—Alliance Missions: Tour of Duty" for strategies to complete the objectives required for each valor medal.

The Silver Cluster

Mission Received: 6

Awarded for saving the *ANS Ulysses*—a civilian transport carrying escaping high-ranking Alliance military and civilian personnel—and its support convoy, from Coalition attack.

The Black Eagle

Mission Received: II

Received for the destruction of the *CS Czar* super carrier—while in its final stages of completion—in a surprise attack. Another component of this mission is safely bringing back a combat team with captured Coalition information stolen from the *Czar*'s docking facility.

Medal of Valor

Mission Received: 14

Awarded for completing a secret long-range operation where the 45th destroys both an advanced Coalition Warp Gate and research facility. The Coalition carrier *CS Krasny* is also destroyed during the attack.

Legion of Service

Mission Received: 17

In a warp attack, the 45th Squadron engages and destroys the Coalition Ion Cannon platform protecting Titan. The valor medal is awarded for the destruction of Dark Reign, a Coalition Ion Cannon.

Navy Cross

Mission Received: 19

Awarded for the rescue of Klaus Steiner, the Alliance's premier ace, from the Coalition prison ship, *Saladin*. During the attack and rescue, the player destroys and kills Kariq Madiz, a known Coalition ace protecting the *Saladin*.

Alliance Medal of Honor

Mission Received: 23

Received for the destruction of the carrier *CS Pukov* and its onboard fighter squadron, the Black Guard, in a set-piece battle with the *Yamato*. The Black Guard and *CS Pukov* have been the principal enemies of the Alliance fleet since the opening days of the conflict.

appendix B

Interview with the *StarLancer* Team

Creating one of the most exciting space combat simulations of all time required many talented individuals. In this interview, you'll get a glimpse into the making of *StarLancer*, including the design team's mission design process, balancing ships and weapons, and the inspirations for the Alliance-Coalition conflict.

We would like to thank the Warthog team, including Paul Hughes (Lead Programmer), Paul Chapman (Interface Designer), Nick Elms (Designer and Team Leader), Phil Meller (Designer and Art Director), Kevin Ng (Programmer), Derek Senior (Programmer), and Phil Mervik (Mission Designer) for their participation in this interview.

The Making of StarLancer

Q: *StarLancer* eschews the usual space combat simulation story of humans versus aliens and instead weaves a tale of a futuristic cold war. How was *StarLancer*'s storyline developed, and were there any particular inspirations?

A: Basically everyone was sick to death of seeing cliché aliens masquerading as bad guys in these types of games. Let's face it, if we do some day meet up with an alien race, they most certainly won't come in the form of a carrier fleet hell bent on wiping out mankind. We're not in the business of pure realism, but I'd rather tag a human foe than some run-of-the-mill alien. With the storyline, we wanted to give it a real sense of desperation—backs to the wall kind of stuff—much like the UK in WW2 when, just after the retreat from Dunkirk, they had to stand and face the might of the all-conquering German army, alone.

Q: What goes into creating an exciting, challenging, and well-balanced single-player mission? What do you take into account, and how do you balance fun and difficulty while keeping it all within the evolving storyline?

A: Concerning the single-player missions in *StarLancer,* we wanted to get away from the blasting, wave-after-wave of incoming-bad-guys type scenarios. However good-looking your game is, gamers will only tolerate this for so long. We've tried to make the missions as diverse and nonlinear as possible. If the player screws up in their objective, the game doesn't come to a complete standstill where you have to replay the mission until you achieve every objective. Instead you can cut your losses and move on to the next mission. Mistakes in earlier missions may come back to haunt you, but that's the gamble you take.

Q: *StarLancer's* user interface is extremely easy-to-use and doesn't crowd the player's view of the action. How did you develop the heads-up display? Were there any features that didn't make it into the game due to design constraints, or any that did despite design constraints?

A: The heads-up display is fairly standard for this type of game. We aimed to create something that looked as if it was being projected back and forth into the pilot's view, like a hologram.

The design and position of elements is based on frequency of use and importance. We strived to include all the best elements of existing space combat sims, along with a few new things like the powerball. The fact that windows time out and close helps to keep the view uncluttered, but you can choose to keep them locked up there. I play the game with hardly any windows open, but some players like to keep track of all their systems.

There are three displays that I think are particularly cool. The missile ring is a great way to select your weapons, and it reminds me of the chamber of a revolver. The enemy target window allows the player to toggle through smaller subtargets on large ships. Destroying these subtargets will affect how that ship acts. The powerball is a cool way of showing distribution of power to systems and feels very interactive when controlled with the joystick.

In terms of what we didn't put in, I would have liked the HUD to have been rendered fully in 3D, with semitransparency, but this is a major frame rate hit, and the processor power is better used to draw more and bigger game objects. In terms of functions, I'm happy with what we have. I've been quite involved in testing, as well, and haven't heard people asking for any extra functions.

Q: Can you explain the design and creation phase for the Alliance and Coalition fighters, particularly their structure and appearance? How were names chosen for each ship? Were there any ships or names that didn't make the final cut?

A: From the outset we wanted the ships to look fully functional—no wacky organic designs as seen in some games/movies. The art team was brought into the WW2 look, and it was agreed that we'd pay homage to this era of aviation history. Alliance fighters would represent the different nations; German fighters had to look bulky, as though they could pack a real punch. The Japanese fighters would be akin to the Zero—graceful and agile but lacking in the armor/firepower department. The US fighters resemble contemporary US fighters—state of the art and real easy on the eye. With the Coalition, fighters' basic functionality is king. A no frills, mass-produced quality was the look we went for—definitely a case of quantity over quality. The naming of the ships was a team effort, and we went with what we thought was appropriate; for example, you automatically associate the Patriot with the US, the Crusader with the British, the Grendel with the Germans, and so on. Concerning ships and ship names that were scrapped, I can hand and heart say that none were scrapped.

Q: In regards to the balancing act between the Alliance fighters, how do you ensure that one fighter isn't better than all the others? Does mission diversity play a role in helping differentiate the ships and nudge the player into selecting a different ship for most missions?

A: We wanted to make a game in which you wouldn't just pick the next available ship and ditch all previous ones. In *StarLancer*, resources are scarce, and each ship has strengths and weaknesses; for example, when a player starts out, they have a choice of four different fighters, all of which have a variety of plus and negative points.

The Predator is light and agile and lightly armored with a fairly low fire rate; however, the Predator's one big plus point is that it has Blind Fire, a self-locking gunnery system, perfect for the novice pilot. On the other hand, purists can opt for the Grendel, a slow and cumbersome craft that packs an awesome amount of fire power. You also have the Crusader, a light fighter that thinks it's a medium one, with its "Spectral Shield" technology giving it limited invulnerability. Finally, there is the Naginata, an extremely light and agile craft ideal for the more discerning pilot who relies more on stealth and speed over sheer brute force.

There will be occasions in which a certain ship's strength could be the difference between failure and success in the mission, and this ship could be one of the starting craft.

Q: What considerations went into creating *StarLancer*'s diverse arsenal of guns and missiles? The missiles function similarly to the different playable fighters. How did you achieve optimal balance and decide upon the missile release schedule?

A: For each ship in *StarLancer*, we have tried to build a custom arsenal specifically tailored to its needs. Many of the ships have different gun combinations that cater to different player styles.

For example, the Mirage fighter is equipped with a powerful Neutron Particle Cannon and twin Messon Blasters. Together these weapons are capable of delivering an extremely destructive blast. However, with both guns operating at the same time, you may only get out two or three bursts before the gun energy is drained. For sharp shooters, this would be more than adequate to destroy almost any fighter, but switching off one of the combinations would reduce energy consumption and allow the "gun jockey" to chase down fighters without worrying too much about not having full power at their fingertips. Another slant on the guns can be levered from the power allocation window, where the play can dynamically alter the amount of power allocated to their ships' systems, giving themselves more gun power at the cost of either engines or shields.

There are fast locking, armor-penetrating missiles that are highly useful in close combat situations. Screamers, on the other hand, take away the automated edge of the lockers and can be fired in abundance and at will. From range, you have to be a real sharp shooter, but up close and personal, they're lethal.

Some utilize the force impact of the blast radius to stun ships, while others short-circuit ships' systems leaving it stranded for a timed period.

As to the timed release of the missiles throughout the course of the game, we wanted to highlight the desperation at the outset of the game. Raw materials are in short supply, and thus missiles are hard to come by. As the game progresses and the Alliance gathers its resources, more and more missiles are made available to the player.

Q: *StarLancer's* beautiful, fast-paced, graphical engine was obviously custom-made for the needs of a space combat simulator. Can you explain some of the ins and outs of the graphical design process and how *StarLancer's* 3D engine caters to the fast-paced action experience?

A: *StarLancer's* graphics engine has been designed on an evolutionary basis. When we started on the engine, the Voodoo1 had only just come out! Our objectives have been twofold. First, make the engine as fast as possible. Tell an artist you can only have 3,000 polygons, and he will assume 6,000! This obviously allows for more detailed ships, as well as a smoother gaming experience. Second, add as many features to make the game look as good as possible. This includes progressive levels of detail, dynamic lighting, alpha blending, environment maps, light maps . . . I could go on. The idea is that if we want to add an effect in the game, the engine would be able to do it. Of course, these features got added as we went along, but because of the flexible nature of the engine, these features were easy to add.

Q: *StarLancer's* context-based music enhances the experience, especially during intense combat situations. Can you elaborate on the musical composition and how important the music was to rounding out the entire gaming experience?

A: There was great emphasis from the outset concerning *StarLancer's* musical score. We wanted a real big, over-the-top cinematic score to accompany every facet of the game. To avoid repetition and enhance the different moods the missions required, 40 unique tracks were required, which were: two launch tracks, one track for enemy space, one track for friendly space, ten searching tracks/precombat tracks, and ten simulation pod tracks. Instead of a big orchestral number, we went for a techno, up-tempo style of music to give the simulation pod a more arcade-type experience. There's one somber track to emote the feeling of loss, and this track might kick in when the player has lost a comrade or when they come across the smouldering hulk of an Alliance craft. Finally, there are four tracks to cater to the various degrees of success achieved in a mission: complete failure, partial failure; partial success, and total success.

Q: Do you plan to release any mission editors or customization tools for *StarLancer*? If so, can you elaborate on them and how you expect the tools to enhance the *StarLancer* experience, particularly the growing online community?

A: Currently we don't have any plans to release our mission editor for two reasons, mainly. First, it would be a nightmare to support it, and second, it would mean someone from the mission design team sitting down and writing a very long document explaining not only its feature set, but also the mission scripting language.

Q: A diverse set of multiplayer games certainly extends the life of any single-player focused game. How were *StarLancer*'s multiplayer deathmatch scenarios designed, and why the inclusion of power-ups? Also, what sorts of changes did you make for the cooperative missions to ensure greater challenge, but not at the expense of maximum enjoyment?

A: The big Achilles' heel of space combat simulation deathmatches is that its participants always end up plodding around in circles trying to outdo each others' turning circle. This really goes hand-in-hand with the fact that there is no architecture to hide behind in space.

Much of our design process for deathmatch was consumed by finding ways to counter this. We achieved this by adding densely packed asteroids and space hulks into the environment, and restricting play by bounding the arena in a spherical force field. Some of the asteroids are huge and have tunnels cut through them to lose your opponents in. We then added powerups. The player can find a way out of a turning battle by collecting a power-up and gaining advantage. The different scenarios in deathmatch also provide different goals and objectives for the player, different ways to kill the opponent.

Cooperative play was a question of time-consuming balancing. We ramp missions up according to the number of players in the session—adding more fighters to increase the difficulty. We found the added challenge made players cooperate more—for example, two players would draw the capital ship's turret fire while the other two concentrated on the fighters.

Q: *StarLancer* already has many online "squadrons," or groups of users devoted to each other, the game, and the online combat experience. How do you see the space combat simulation evolving in an online gaming world?

A: It's a genre people have attempted to tap into, but one that doesn't seem to have been fully exploited. This is something we're hoping to rectify with *StarLancer*. It's a real compliment that people have already set up online squadrons before the game is even finished. We're hoping that people find the cooperative play as rewarding as the deathmatch play.